ANNI & CARSTEN SENNOV

SPIRIT MATES

HOW TO FIND YOUR SOUL MATE VERSION 2.0
YOUR ULTIMATE LOVE PARTNER

With 10 Real Life Love Stories

good adventures publishing

SPIRIT MATES

HOW TO FIND YOUR SOUL MATE VERSION 2.0
YOUR ULTIMATE LOVE PARTNER

©2019, Anni & Carsten Sennov and Good Adventures Publishing
First edition, first impression
Set with Cambria
Layout: Anni Sennov – www.good-adventures.com
Cover design: Michael Bernth – www.monovoce.dk
Photos for Love Story #6 and #7 from private collections
Painting for Love Story # 8 by Francois Dupuis
Reproduced with permission by the artist
Author photo, cover photo and all other photos in the book:
Aamod & Sophelia Korhonen – www.balanceisjoy.com

Proofread and edited by: Aislinn Gagliardi – www.aislinngagliardi.com
8 love stories translated from Swedish into English by:
Linda Larsson – www.lindaslinguistics.com

ISBN 978-87-7206-082-8

Contents

Notice

When reading this book, please be in a spirit of open-mindedness.

Although the authors and the publisher have made every effort to ensure the accuracy and completeness of information contained in this book, they assume no responsibility for errors, inaccuracies, omissions or any inconsistencies herein. Any offense caused to people, places or organizations is unintentional.

Readers should use their own judgment or consult a holistic medical expert or their personal physician for specific applications to their individual problems.

In this book AuraTransformation™ is mentioned several times.

AuraTransformation™ is an energy treatment method that was founded by Anni Sennov in 1996. It's a permanent spiritual expansion of your aura and consciousness, and it activates the spirit's journey into your body.

It's much more likely for most aura-transformed adults, and for today's children and young adults born from 1995 onwards, to meet their Spirit Mate, than it is for people at soul level. This is because at soul level, your energies only allow you the potential for a Soul Mates relationship, whereas with today's children and young adults and all aura-transformed people, they have a Crystal or Indigo aura that consists of pure spirit energy, and which allows the potential for them to have a Spirit Mates relationship instead.

Many aura-transformed people say that they doubt they

would have met their Spirit Mate if they had not had an Aura-Transformation™, but it's not a prerequisite for meeting your Spirit Mate.

If you want to know more about AuraTransformation™ and how to upgrade your aura to spirit level, please visit **www.auratransformation.com**.

Introduction

Many books have been written about love and how it feels to fall in love and be in love. This book is different!

This book will inspire you and bring hope deep into your heart that there is a one and only Spirit Mate for you somewhere out there.

You will get to know how it is to **be and feel love** in all its aspects when being together with your *Spirit Mate*, aka your *Soul Mate version 2.0* and *Your One and Only*.

You will get a deep understanding of what it is that is so unique about your Spirit Mate that will allow you to completely open your heart to a "stranger" whom you just met. You will also learn what it is that causes two people to suddenly connect with each other deep in their hearts with no filter between them, so they are unable to ever separate their energies from each other again.

Many answers will be given to you when you read the 10 amazing real-life Spirit Mates love stories that we share in this book, and then you will also know why there is **nothing** you can do other than to surrender to love, when your one and only true love finally comes knocking on the door to your heart.

But how can you know if this person is your Spirit Mate?

Well, besides the insight from the love stories in this book and our guidance, it's really only you and your love partner who will know for sure that you are Spirit Mates, since it's a very special feeling and so different from any previous relationships you've had.

All couples who have stepped forward to share their unique love stories in this book have felt this, and we are so grateful that they have agreed to share their very personal love stories with our readers.

From the depths of our hearts, we wish for you that you will find your one and only Spirit Mate if that is what you wish for, because everybody deserves to come home ♡ ♡ ♡

Anni & Carsten Sennov

Most people have a deep longing in their hearts

Most people have a deep longing for love in their hearts, whether it's a longing to be reunited with their God and their spiritual source, or it's a longing to merge together with their one and only love partner in physical life. There might of course be other things that people long for, but the one and only common denominator to connecting with God and your spiritual source, and with your one and only spiritual love partner, is that they represent unconditional love in a pure form.

Most people on Earth are longing for pure and unconditional love, and they often search for it throughout their life. Only when they have connected with God and their spiritual source or with their Spirit Mate and their one and only love partner, can they then relax and stop chasing love. Why is that?

It's simply because they have become pure love themselves, which is radiated and reflected in everything they do, and it makes them feel more comfortable and much stronger on a personal level, than they have ever felt before. It's like everything in life suddenly makes sense on a much higher level and they feel that they can survive anything because they have now met themselves and their own energy in another person, or because they have connected to the highest Love Source.

When unconditional love becomes an integrated part of your daily life by either connecting with God or merging your energy with the energy of your Spirit Mate, infinity becomes an essential part of your everyday life on a very physical and human level, and the purpose of living becomes so much more obvious than ever before.

Losing love creates vulnerability

Those who constantly search for love usually feel very vulnerable deep inside, because they feel that they have failed to find true love. However, love is not supposed to be found outside of yourself. You must be able to love yourself unconditionally so that others can love you in the same way. Self-love, not to be confused with selfishness, is therefore important in any serious love relationship.

If you love others more than you love and appreciate yourself, there can never be balance in the relationship. You must be able to embrace love in your life, and love yourself as much as you love others, and unconditionally. Not only one party in a relationship should be loved unconditionally, as love is meant for everyone, including you. The love energy goes both ways, and if you are not being loved unconditionally by your partner, you should for sure be loved unconditionally by yourself, so you can start making the right decisions in your life that reflect your love for yourself.

The day that you are able to love yourself unconditionally, and thereby be able to embrace yourself and your life with love, is the day that you can stop searching for your one and only love parter. Be sure that he/she will be just around the corner and meet you as soon as you accept and welcome the unconditional love that comes from him/her into your life. The presence of pure love in your life, however, can be quite a big mouthful for both of you to digest on a personal, emotional and spiritual level, because how are you supposed to react when all your prayers are suddenly heard and fulfilled?

Pure and unconditional love between two conscious and responsible adults can be absolutely magnificent, but it can also be overwhelming and tough to deal with in everyday life, since the life perspective of you and your love partner is suddenly changed from "I" to "We," which is a 180-degree rotation in everything you do, think and feel.

Often big decisions and radical changes have to be made in a very short time, as a daily separation between you and your love partner may feel like a knife stabbed into your heart, if you cannot be together as much as you like. This can be hard for a love couple to deal with, and it can be even harder for a love couple if they have children from previous relationships.

Since most parents love their children in the same unconditional way as they love their new spiritual love partner, and they want to take optimal care of the children and protect them, it's not always possible to move in together within the first weeks and create a totally new family life together. There can be many factors to consider, if you have children, parents, other family and friends, or work, other relationships or activities that mean a lot to you, because they must of course be taken into account when you and your Spirit Mate are planning your new life together. During the first phase of any Spirit Mates relationship, patience and trust are therefore going to be your best friends. Not just trust in your new love partner, but trust in life.

How did Spirit Mates come about?

Your Spirit Mate and your twin flame is the other part of your spiritual energy from which you both originated, on a consciousness level, back in the beginning of time, at the moment of the great cosmic cell division.

Spirit duality can thus be traced back considerably further in the history of consciousness development than soul energy. It corresponds to the spiritual interconnectedness between two cells and/or two people coming from the same cell division.

In the great cosmic cell division, every cell divided into two cells at a time, usually in the form of a masculine and a feminine energy which together represent a spiritual duality. It is this cell division which is now being restored to its spiritual source by the couple being brought together as love partners in their earthly lives.

Spirit Mates have exactly the same consciousness structure and platform by virtue of their common origin in the spirit.

Spirit Mates may well have met each other already at the soul level, but due to a partial or missing connection with the spiritual dimension they were not yet whole and in full balance both in themselves and in the relationship. Therefore, the couple was not able to jointly exploit the full potential of their relationship, which, further along the way, will lead to their common mission in life revealing itself.

Spirit Mates have a deep, inner love for each other and often an inexplicable sense of cohesion that is not granted to Soul Mates. The Soul Mates relationship is subject to external conditions in relation to certain earthly life paths and specific life tasks. However, this does not mean that Soul Mates cannot love each other deeply.

Out in the cosmos there is no such thing as soul energy and soul partnership. They are purely earthly phenomena whereas spirituality and spirit duality are not. Meeting your Spirit Mate on a physical level and starting to merge your energies here on Earth is therefore a clear sign that you have both come to the next level relationship-wise where you are able to connect on a much higher level both in spirit and in person. This is the case whether it's happening with your existing soul partner or with a new love partner.

In the next chapter you can read the very first Spirit Mates love story that we have decided to share with you in this book. It's an absolutely unique and at the same time very touching and tough story of how many challenges a Spirit Mates love couple, who love each other unconditionally, are able to go through together in their relationship and come out even stronger on the other side. The most amazing part of the whole story is that today the love couple sees all the challenges they have been through as a divine gift that helped them get even closer to each other on all levels. On their way towards this unique state of divinity in the relationship, they managed to get rid of toxic stuff from their past in a very profound and cleansing way.

We are proud to say that we actually have their wedding photo hanging in our house, in Anni's consultation room, because Anna and Ola were one of the first Spirit Mates couples we heard of that got married. Anna is holding the bridal bouquet in a victorious way in her right arm over her head and Ola, her newly wedded husband, is holding her left hand while having his left arm around his daughter on the other side. It's unbelievable how much love, power and embracement there is in that photo.

Ola and Anna

Love Story # 1

Anna says: From the moment I first saw Ola, when he opened the door to the osteopathic clinic, I thought he was very special. His presence and his appearance caught all my attention. A friend and therapist had warmly recommended him when I was looking for an osteopath. I was affected in many ways by our first meeting; he radiated wisdom and greatness, and he had books in his bookcase that had revolutionized my life. Our conversation had a deep meaning from the first moment.

But I was so convinced that he was married, that I never thought of him as being available. In addition, I could see the humor in becoming interested in one's therapist. I was simply a grateful patient for fantastic treatments and delightful conversations.

I had just recently moved back to Skåne, Sweden after many years abroad. I had passed age 35 a while back and the only thing I wished for was to find a husband and build a family. For a while, my longing was so strong that I got in my own way. It took me a couple of years of searching and finding; psychosynthesis studies and yoga teacher studies that led up to me doing an AuraTransformation™. This gave me a completely new stability in everything I had found along my way. During my AuraTransformation™ I knew that I must do the Aura Mediator Course. At the same time I started to change my outlook on life; I began to feel satisfied with being alone and decided that even if I never meet someone, I will live a rich life. However, my crystallization (Crystal energy upgrade in the body) was so intensive and so fast that I needed help with my body to keep up. There was even more to talk about with Dr. Ola and he became so interested in AuraTransformation™ that we decided to exchange treatments.

Ola says: The first time I met Anna was as my patient. It felt as though she was in the middle of her life and bursting with energy. I had to make an effort to stay focused when Anna told me, among other things, that she was going to the jungles of Costa Rica to practice yoga. A trip to my taste. I realized that Anna was also to my taste when I reflected on our meeting. But having worked with patients for over twenty-five years, and never inviting anything other than professional contact, it didn't feel particularly natural to do it this time either.

I let fate determine, or rather, I hoped with trust that we would meet again. Perhaps somewhere other than the treatment room? Fate wanted it. That we would meet. Though still in the treatment room. Six months later.

A short time before this meeting I had finally – I thought – given up on meeting my great love. A divorce, and relationships that had ended afterwards, had led me to a decision to give up on intimate love relationships for good. Or rather: I would stop searching for them. I would sell my house, and buy a farm in the country. Start off by living for a month in a monastery by myself. The farm would be a great base for me and my daughter's continued life. I felt peaceful. After years of searching, among other places with the shamans in Mexico and the aborigines in Australia, I felt more and more at home in myself.

Just as the last time I met Anna, I was charmed. I loved listening to her speak; speak about exciting things like AuraTransformation™. At the end of the treatment I heard myself say that I was interested in that type of treatment.

Anna says: Ola's AuraTransformation™ was something completely different. I had only seen him from a patient's perspective; he was the grounded therapist. When I put my hands on his feet I was so surprised, I didn't expect this enormous power and dynamics. I recognized a bubbling feeling that I can experience in myself and thought it was strange to recognize my own energy in someone else. We laughed out loud for half an hour just from the energies. I had never even been close to a heart of his size. I left the treatment forever changed, but of course I kept it to myself. When he sent a text a week later and asked if we could see a movie by a favorite author that we both shared, it was as if I burnt myself on the phone; I had to throw it away from me. Crazy.

When we met again there was no going back. Ola's Aura-Transformation™ was on the 8th of April. In June we left for Santorini in Greece together, where he proposed. In July we became pregnant, and then we married on the 10th of the 10th of the 10th (October 10, 2010). It felt as if our meeting was arranged even before we met. That's why everything could move so very fast. Despite the pace, I felt a huge comfort in that Ola didn't "need" me. He had everything he needed; he didn't need to be coached, which was something I had done in every which way in all of my previous relationships. Since I had come into my own happiness right before we met, I really didn't "need" him either.

Ola says: When this beautiful woman held me during the treatment it felt like coming home. To be seen totally. The treatment meant that my heart began to expand to its full potential again. I also began to find it easier to make decisions in different everyday matters. Matters which I had tediously been thinking about for far too long. Weighted for or against. Now, suddenly, I felt as if I had full access to my instincts.

The more we met, the more I realized how alike we were and how we had the same interests. Of course, I invited her shortly thereafter for a coffee and a movie by and about one of our favorite authors. We didn't watch much of the movie and I dropped my plans of going into a monastery.

It was as if a large wild force had seized hold of me. There was no doubt. We were us. It felt like I had no choice at all. Thankfully.

Two months later I went to Santorini to visit Anna. It was a volcanic experience! I proposed to her there. We were married after a few more months. Anna was already carrying our first son.

Anna says: Matteo was born in April of the following year. Then came a year of enjoyment and adjustment before we became pregnant again and our second son was born. When our first son was three years old and our second son was nine months old the unthinkable happened. Our three year old son was diagnosed with acute lymphocytic leukemia (ALL). We were thrown all the way to hell and back during the two and a half years of treatment. Suffering of this caliber is a very effective way to clear out everything unnecessary. Unnecessary things that many times were manifested as difficult passages between us; everything came up to the surface. We were tested to extremes and with that we were thrown, for the first time, in different directions in our different reactions. But since our focus the entire time was on our son meeting his challenge in the best way, we had the same fundamental objective and could therefore act as a unit despite everything. It was as if we, with the diagnosis, stood in diametrically different places and, during the suffering, moved towards the same goal to finally meet again, in an even more total way.

On the whole we have had very little time of our own; we are always together as a family with the children. So it's in the meeting with the family that we have also had to meet as a couple.

Ola says: It was as if we were on an Orient Express which, with dizzying speed made stop-overs, or "spiritual stops," at the most fantastic stations; like when our two sons were born and when we bought our house, the train suddenly took another track. We traveled through an enchanted landscape, only to violently crash straight into a cold and hard iron curtain. I initially experienced it as such when the news came that our beloved Matteo was suffering from leukemia. At the same time as Anna blew into another state of consciousness, a sort of expanded consciousness, I had to fight in order to just stand up. This was the first time that I felt like we were on different tracks, but at the same time it was as if we could see each other; as if the trains were moving in the same direction. I could at least see Anna. I knew she was in a kind of enlightened state of mind.

As the diagnosis blew her into another dimension – which I usually called "eagle's gift" – that I had practiced for as long as I can remember, I experienced the situation instead as medieval torture. I felt like a professional boxer who suddenly could not switch off my practiced combinations.

Paralyzed by the hell of seeing my son suffer without being able to ease it, I had to take a kind of detour – a side track – where I accepted the hell and took every little ray of light as a victory. I also realized that I was neither cursed nor blessed but instead only challenged. After three weeks I rose like a warrior and accepted the challenge. What happened with Anna during this journey is worth its own book and it has been written. By Anna. In the midst of this inferno. With the title: "The Hidden Gifts of Cancer," or "Cancerns Gömda Gåvor" in Swedish.

Today, our son is fully healthy and has recovered from the tough treatment that ended in the fall of 2016. He is beautiful and seems very wise for his age.

Anna says: The main difference from all other relationships is that it was, and is, so clear that we are us. There is no doubt or uncertainty. Our connection is so complete that there is no space where we don't connect. Just like a full screen reflection; I can see every pinky and every hair in the reflection. In previous relationships, I might have seen a hand, an arm, or at best, a head. But, this complete place of connection is clearly not *only* easy. The shadow side is also reflected and the pain is as complete as the love when we go through difficulties. When we go through a difficult phase, suffering is very real, but I always have trust deep down and the knowledge that this will soon pass. The humor in this is that when Ola irritates me and wants to point out *how* I am irritating, it's *exactly that* which irritates me about him. In other words, we have the same shortcomings or very similar ones anyways. Everything is visible in the mirror!

In all other relationships I have had secret rooms. Things that I simply have not shared or wished to have someone else's view on. But even if I search within myself I can't find anything that I don't share with Ola. He knows everything. Since Ola also feels everything there was a time in the beginning when he could be irritated that I judged him, before I knew it myself. I would not have realized exactly what irritated me, but he would already know that he was under the magnifying glass and being judged. He immediately knows how I feel. Everything is visible, nothing can be hidden and it puts great demands on us. We have to hold on to our own deep inner balance; if we don't do that, it will affect not only us as individuals but most of all, even us as a couple.

Ola says: Between us there is a kind of equality or balance of which I have never come close to in any previous love relationship. There is usually no resistance at all; we live in a flow where my desires coincide with hers. I don't need to be someone I'm not, or go against any of my instincts to satisfy her needs, as they coincide with my own. There is no drama – unless I am the one to create it – and instead I can fully be myself even if we see each other every day. It's as if there is really no distortion at all.

Our everyday life begins more and more to mean that we work together, like on different book projects. I like working at my medical clinic, but sometimes it feels a bit unnatural that we don't work together there more also. Though we have started seeing mutual patients, which is to say that I treat certain patients as an osteopath and then they see Anna in her role as an Aura Mediator™.

I used to think it was actually dangerous to a couple to work together; because you could get tired of each other and not have anything to talk about. For us it feels the opposite, our relationship just gets more exciting and enjoyable the more we see each other.

I don't feel like we are together because we complement each other so well. We don't need to. We have our basic happiness and basic trust anyways. We are each of us complete on our own. Instead we are together because our spirits want us to be. Because it's wonderful and natural.

On the other hand, this doesn't necessarily mean that we never encounter resistance. To so totally be able to reflect oneself in another person doesn't always mean that it's easy. The reflection means that you can never hide behind empty phrases or quasi-intellectual reasoning.

When it sometimes storms between us, we remind ourselves of something that Rumi, our favorite philosopher, has said:

"Out beyond ideas of wrongdoing
and rightdoing is a field.
I'll meet you there."

My other half sees "straight through me." I must be "me," that is to say completely authentic. Sometimes I have to make an effort to be "just me" for our sake; for my sake. There really lies a great comfort in it. It should be easy. Yet I must often remind myself that I am good enough exactly as I am.

If I don't take care of myself there will be consequences for the relationship greater than I have ever been through before. To "honor Anna" in this reflecting relationship I must also "honor" myself.

In other relationships that I have had over the past 26 years, I also always felt that close relationships were relative compromises; compromises with myself to make twosomeness even possible. This caused me, with a certain regularity, to need to get away on my own to find my way home to myself again. That is never the case in this very special love story because I am myself, and fully my own spirit, even when I am with Anna. Instead, all my dreams are about how I could have even more time together with her. That feeling only continues to grow.

Anna says: I didn't just get Ola, but also his daughter from his first marriage. The funny thing is that we also have a strong spiritual connection. We are really no coincidence and she fits very well together with her little brothers. Everything fits; I even like the daughter's mother. We have a good relationship and respect each other. The rest of the family blends together in some ways unusually well. The first time I met Ola's mother tears ran on both of us, as if we knew each other from somewhere else. It's the same with my family and Ola. We are very close in my family, and we see each other often, but it's never a problem, as Ola likes when my family is close. Sometimes Ola expresses his surprise, as he has a high integrity and it's new for him to be so close to the family.

Everyday life with two small children and a teenager is very intense. Thankfully, we agree on most things. Purely structural we choose the same routines for our children and for ourselves. This also applies to leisure and culture; if we want to see a movie, it tends to be quite easy to choose one that we both appreciate. It's the same with music and literature. The funny thing is that we don't only like the same things in everything, but when we really like something, we usually share it 100%. Another example of this is interior decorating, which we both are very entertained by. When we consider and plan the interior of a room, we sometimes think differently, but when we really love something, it's always the same thing. We've learned to wait until everything falls together perfectly because then we unite and all is right.

We long to work together more. Just before we had our first son, I left the business world to open my own yoga studio. But the leukemia intervened and helped me find a great part of my life's mission, that of cancer rehabilitation. As Ola had written before I started writing, I received great support in what the process entails. In fact, it was thanks to my husband that I began writing at all. Our journey through the leukemia became a book about the hidden gifts that cancer brought to us; it was very comforting to hold a hand during the entire process. We gladly write together. Each one individually, but we sit in the same time and space. When we devote ourselves to shared projects our dynamics are amplified, and when we totally dedicate our intent on the same goal, it feels as if we receive help from another dimension. Boundaries are erased, and that which was separated: relationship, work and leisure, has a completely new way of blending together into a single platform.

The only tips we could ever give on optimizing the possibility of meeting your Spirit Mate, is to fully land in yourself and your own spirit. Follow your inner compass and make sure that your choices are authentic and not based on any influence from any other person. It seems that the probability of meeting someone who has found their own treasure chest increases radically when you yourself have found the road to your own treasure.

Unconditional Love

As you can understand from reading Anna and Ola's love story, your Spirit Mate is the most beautiful person, in all ways, that you have ever known. You feel completely whole, strong and rested in your own energy as well as in your common energy when the two of you are together. Unconditional love, freedom and trust is the foundation in any Spirit Mates relationship.

When you give up searching for love outside of yourself and you accept and decide to live a happy, balanced and joyful life on your own terms where you love yourself without chasing external love, then you become peaceful inside, and this is radiated in your aura and personal appearance. You may even consider becoming a nun or a monk and live in a convent or monastery for the rest of your life. If so, then you know that you have finally accepted to not compromise when it comes to love. This is the only way for you to open your heart to your one and only Spirit Mate and divine love partner.

When you are together with your Spirit Mate and you both focus on the same matter, cause or situation, the energy in and around you is raised to a much higher spiritual level. This is always the case when you both follow your inner GPS and agree on where to go. If only one of you wants to head for a certain goal, you might have to work harder to reach the goal unless you are fully supported by your love partner.

If you head for different goals, there won't be any resistance coming from your Spirit Mate, and no compromises are made either in you or in your relationship. If you agree to go in different directions with certain matters, you will both do it in a way that leaves room for both of you to succeed, each in your own way.

You can always be yourself as you truly are and in everything you do, say, think and feel in your Spirit Mates love relationship. Even though you're not together in everything you do on a daily basis, you always cooperate with each other to ease life for your love partner, simply because it feels so complete, beautiful and natural for both of you to support each other. So when you forget to think of yourself and your own needs, you can be sure that your Spirit Mate will think of you just like you would think of him/her in a similar situation.

Spirit Mates have the exact same profound wishes and needs in life, and therefore it feels so right to always try to fulfill your partner's wishes, because then you automatically fulfill your own wishes and needs without even focusing on it. Similar to Ola's analogy from Love Story # 1, it's like two trains heading for the same station at the same time driving on two different tracks, where they can always see and communicate clearly with each other on all levels.

Spirit Mates have an unconditional acceptance of each other through their common spiritual source and their identical consciousness. Love, trust, confidence and intuition are their common key words in the relationship, and they never doubt each other's deepest intentions in any given situation. You might just as well doubt your own intentions, since you both get your spiritual impulses from the same spiritual platform.

The individual balance is equally as important as the mutual balance in the relationship. If you don't allow room for your partner to find themselves, there will be no room for you in the relationship to find yourself, as you mirror each other in everything you do, think, feel and say. There is absolutely no way back when you finally meet and connect on a physical level, because you recognize yourself in everything your partner does. It feels like coming home, so why should you forbid each other to do certain things if you love each other unconditionally and have positive intentions in everything you do in relation to each other?

People who limit and violate each other are for sure not Spirit Mates.

The difference between
Soul Mates and Spirit Mates

Soul Mates

The term Soul Mate, also called your Twin Soul, has been used for decades to describe a relationship between two people who have a deep love connection at soul level.

A relationship between two Soul Mates represents an energy constellation between two often fundamentally different spiritual beings who, for reasons of consciousness development on Earth, have agreed to get together as love partners through several physical incarnations and therefore have a strong magnetic attraction to each other.

The soul partnership allows the two parties to feel bound to each other by fate despite maybe having great basic personal differences, but it can also be karmic life connections and unresolved business between the two that bind them together.

The sphere of the soul is contained within the sphere of the spirit, and it has a connection to the Earth's previous reincarnation and karma system, where various personal relationships between people are agreed upon from one life to the next.

When people have the conviction that they are connected with a particular person on the level of soul and destiny, it does not feel nearly as difficult for either of them to acquire personal skills and qualities that come from the other person's consciousness universe, even though these qualities may differ dramatically from their own original energy structure.

Soul energy is on the decline here on Earth, as all children from 1995 onwards have been born with only pure spirit energy in their aura. At this period in time, soul energy is therefore solely related to older generations born prior to 1995.

Consciousness Mates

Not many people know about the phenomenon called Consciousness Mates, as it is a relatively modern way of developing your personal skills through a close relationship with another person.

Consciousness Mates may be of either sex, where the relationship presents itself as either a deep friendship or most often as a brief and very intense love affair that ends in nothing.

A Consciousness Mates relationship differs from a Spirit Mates relationship in that it is not absolutely sexually and physically focused. The sexual "plug-and-socket" effect that makes the Spirit Mates' two bodies meld their respective spirit consciousnesses together into one shared spirit energy, is not found in Consciousness Mates, since their original spirit consciousnesses are not completely identical. However, a Spirit Mates relationship is not just purely sexual.

Consciousness Mates are not identical in spirit. In the earthly sphere, even very small differences can separate Consciousness Mates from each other, sometimes in unpleasant and negative ways which may be totally disproportionate to the size of the differences. This can often be followed by great personal pain for both parties because they really want to open up to each other, but apparently cannot, despite their strong desire to do so.

The consciousness duality problem can be likened to attempting to open a door with a key that is cut slightly wrong. The lock simply doesn't fit no matter how much you jiggle the key, as it is simply not the right key that you are trying to use.

Said in a simplified way, Consciousness Mates complement each other on a consciousness level and that is what the relationship is all about: complementing each other during a certain phase of life with the purpose of developing certain skills that the other part possesses.

Soul energy and consciousness duality represent only a small step on the earthly path of development in the individual quest to become one with your total consciousness and its pure spiritual energy, and to finally be united with your ultimate Spirit Mate in both body and spirit.

The level of consciousness at which Consciousness Mates find themselves when they meet is always the same, hence the name and the reason for their meeting. However, the composition of their respective consciousnesses and their life values are not the same.

Spirit Mates have exactly the same life values, and consciousness structure and platform by virtue of their common origin in the spirit.

The Soul Mate, the Consciousness Mate and the Spirit Mates relationships each represent different kinds of development between the two parties in the relationship. However, it can easily happen that a person has one and the same Soul Mate and Spirit Mate, or one and the same Soul Mate and Consciousness Mate. However, people never have the same Consciousness Mate and Spirit Mate.

Spirit Mates may well have met each other already at the soul level without being able to jointly exploit the full potential of their relationship.

Consciousness Mates and Spirit Mates can be difficult to distinguish from each other because they are energetically much more in synchrony with each other than are Soul Mates and Spirit Mates. The quickest way to identify which kind of relationship it is, is by observing how quickly imbalances arise in the relationship. In a Spirit Mates relationship, it is in fact extremely difficult to disagree about anything at all, whereas there are often both small and large disagreements between Consciousness Mates due to them seeing things differently.

Spirit Mates

A person's Spirit mate corresponds to the other part of the person's own spiritual energy and consciousness experience pool with whom they were originally united from the beginning.

The reason why many Spirit Mates couples have just recently started to meet each other as love partners around the globe is pretty obvious, as it is hard work for many people to find a way into themselves. If they have not yet achieved balance and settled down with their own personality, it can be difficult, on a day to day basis, living with a copy of yourself who is constantly highlighting aspects of yourself that you have not yet been completely reconciled with.

Seeing your own personal characteristics played out in real life through another person can feel extremely confrontational, since we can only experience ourselves from the inside out, and not the other way around.

The precondition for the Spirit Mates being allowed to meet each other at all in the earthly sphere is that they both feel whole inside and are in full balance within themselves. Only by being fully in balance with themselves can they be ready at the consciousness level to be united with their Spirit Mate who must also be whole inside and fully balanced. If not, both parties will be held back in their respective spheres of consciousness until it is the right time for them to unite.

For Spirit Mates who have already met at soul level, a huge clean-up is nearly always needed in the relationship when each party becomes complete and comes into full harmony with themselves. They suddenly have to look at each other and their relationship with new eyes, within the context of pure spirit energy.

Often there may have been infidelity, trust issues or other unpleasant experiences in the soul level relationship so that the couple has been forced to break with their original vision of each other. Even if both parties are just as much Spirit Mates and have been from the very beginning, their relationship usually cannot expand from soul level into being a relationship based on spirit duality without getting help from the outside world.

The elements missing in the relationship between the two Soul Mates, so that each can become whole and meet as Spirit Mates, need to come from somewhere. This often takes place through either spiritual or physical infidelity or deep emotional involvement in other people, where one or both parties in the relationship enter into a close relationship with one or more Consciousness Mates on their path in the form of love affairs or deep friendships. An extensive cleaning process is therefore necessary in the relationship so that the Spirit Mates couple can raise their energies together and meet and live on a new and much higher frequency level in daily life.

If Spirit Mates have met as Soul Mates at soul level, they must be able to meet on a whole new basis of joint consciousness, founded on unconditional love, with no grudges or skeletons in the closet from the past.

Be prepared to develop together

Understandably, it takes a lot of effort and time on a personal level for two Spirit Mates' respective consciousnesses to fuse together, so they can leave the soul level and become one in spirit and mind on a spiritual level. However, the history of human evolution has now come to a point where it is time for more individuals to consciously and spiritually begin to unite with the other part of themselves, which is located in another body often of the opposite sex, but not necessarily, as spirit duality is not gender-specific.

All people have a Spirit Mate, and each of us have an imprint of our Spirit Mate in us. Now it is finally possible to create a consciousness and love-based attraction between two Spirit Mate bodies, which outwardly looks like a plug and a socket that fit perfectly together.

Spirit Mates have an innate mutual sense of unity and an unconditional acceptance of each other and they basically agree on everything in their everyday lives. They each have their own approach to life due to their often very different life experiences, which is most obvious at the beginning of the relationship. If an issue should come up for debate, they will quickly reach agreement.

Spirit Mates each come from their individual place in life, but not from their own individual place in consciousness. At spirit level, they are located in exactly the same place and have always been connected with each other in their inner core.

Every human being, either consciously or unconsciously, longs to meet their Spirit Mate – the person with whom they originated in the spirit and who is completely identical to them in the structure of their being. However, most people at soul level seem to get turned on by their opposites, by the qualities of another person that they do not already possess themselves.

When you are not in balance, you will usually focus on things outside of yourself, like for example finding someone who has other skills that you don't have.

When you are in balance, you don't "need" to find someone to supplement you. Instead an inner sense of belonging to your other half is brought to life.

When the two Spirit Mate bodies come into contact with each other, they can generate a great deal of extra energy for their joint benefit, as well as bringing the Spirit Mates' two identical consciousnesses together into one larger joint consciousness energy. In this way, the Spirit Mates may jointly feel even more whole as a couple than they have ever felt as individuals, because love is constantly flowing freely between them, and because they know deep in their heart that they can never be separated from each other again.

If, however, you have already met as a love couple at soul level, be prepared to develop together in the relationship whether you like it or not. Alternatively, you will both have to develop on a personal level through one or more other relationships before you finally meet as a love couple at spirit level.

It can take years for love couples to meet at spirit level and therefore many Spirit Mates have already met each other at soul level even without knowing it, so they could avoid experiencing the very deep feeling of loneliness that most people have deep inside when they have not yet met their Spirit Mate in real life. So even if you don't want to go through the challenging transition from soul level to spirit level that many love couples go through, you may end up preferring that, instead of waiting three more years or even longer to meet your one and only Spirit Mate, who might not be that perfect and/or in perfect balance when you meet him/her, because some personal development is still lacking for him/her to be in balance on a personal level.

In the next Spirit Mates love story, you can read about Sophelia and Aamod, the spiritual photographer couple who have taken nearly all the photos in this book. They met each other at soul level where everything looked nice on the surface, but wasn't.

They loved each other deeply and still do, but the trust was missing. Not only the trust in each other but the trust in themselves, which caused tremendous pain in the relationship. Read their story and get a deep understanding of why it's so important to first and foremost trust yourself and your own intuition instead of always listening to others', even if it's your one and only Spirit Mate you're talking to.

Aamod and Sophelia

Love Story # 2

Sophelia: We met for the first time in the spring of 2008 at a course center for personal development.

We met in a hug and even then I had a very strong and unusual experience in our first meeting. We stood for a long time and hugged each other and I felt that we fused in energy in a way that I had never felt before. There was a kind of recognition in the energy. I was deeply moved, and the energy didn't release after we finished the hug, but I felt that parts of Aamod's energy stayed with me.

Aamod also experienced a strong feeling at this moment. But at that time he wasn't as receptive to experiencing and feeling energy; he was accustomed to using his mind.

A few days later, we met again and had physical contact and held each other's hand. The energy exchange between us was so intense; it felt like time stood still. We experienced an energy healing that rushed around in our bodies. We found it hard to let go of each other. We were dazed after that powerful meeting and life felt different for us afterwards. We met again two weeks later.

Aamod: We lived far apart and we both had the other in our thoughts. We felt each other in a way that is hard to put into words. I went to visit Sophelia and from then on we were a couple and we moved in together.

It felt like coming home to both of us. We felt a fusion and calm come over us and for the first few years we just lay and hugged each other almost 24 hours a day. We didn't get very much practical done, except for just the essentials.

Fortunately, Sophelia already had three children, which meant that we had contact with the outside world. It felt natural for me to be together with all three children and they felt the same way with me. From the very beginning, there was an unspoken feeling of family and a close interconnectedness between all of us. There was a long time of healing and development.

Sophelia: We worked intensively with our personal development and with various forms of therapy, to take care of us and to integrate our new life situation.

We had a lot of joy and love between us, but there was still a huge imbalance in our relationship. It was I who had to stand for a lot of the drive and presence in the personal and spiritual development for both of us, and even in daily life. Aamod took care of the practical things in the home and in the family. Those first years he stayed home and learned to relate to the children, be part of a family, and to be a role model for the children. This was a big change and a long-awaited challenge for him because his life had been deeply isolated, growing up as an only child. Now he trained himself to open up and invite other people in on a deeper level.

I let go of home and children after many years as a stay-at-home mom to go out into the community and start working again. It was a great relief for me to have drawn Aamod to me, he longed so deeply for involvement in the children's and my lives, and we have thrived greatly together from the start. We have different backgrounds and experiences. Nevertheless, we have very similar basic outlooks and values and we had the same priorities concerning development and intimacy.

Aamod: However, I had long since decided never to marry... I saw it as closing in and restricting life. Also I didn't have any positive role models and had experiences of destructive relationships.

Sophelia, however, was not at all interested in destructiveness and worked all the time trying to find a way in to even more creativity, both in her own life and in our relationship. She set boundaries on the destructivity; both in her own life and in mine. I experienced a very strong love and affection for Sophelia that I had never experienced with anyone else. It was mutual.

This meant that I quickly began to change my mind about what a marriage and a deeper relationship could lead to. My decision to never "tie myself down" transformed into a sense of possibilities, development and freedom. After two years, we wrote our own prenuptial joint agreements and decided to get married.

But as the years went by, the imbalances between us became increasingly clear. I was very much up into the Air element/the intellect. I easily lost presence and my grounding, and found it difficult to get in contact with my feelings and guidance from my source/truth. I had to work hard with expressive therapy to be able to keep in contact with myself and had to struggle every day to hold onto my presence, as well as to have an openness to the flow and the energies. It was a necessity, but very energy and time consuming maintaining this in my life, because the effect waned quickly and I felt that I was taking two steps forward and one backward. It was hard and exhausting work, and a great challenge to continue moving forward in order not to fall back into old patterns of isolation and energy bonds to mood, emotions, other people and past experiences.

We made several clear agreements in the relationship, as I have a history of abuse. This was a support so that it would be safer for Sophelia to let me even deeper into her life and so that we wouldn't create unconscious co-dependencies or imbalances in our relationship.

The years passed and we continued with different forms of therapy and surrounded ourselves with open conversation circles that we created with people we felt safe with. This included the whole family and only adult circles with close friends.

Sophelia: In time I started to receive intuitive messages through my emotional system and dreams that something wasn't right between us. Aamod had increasing difficulty in opening up and inviting me in and breaking his deep isolation. I asked several times and shared my sense of worry and discomfort and asked Aamod if he was still keeping his part of the agreements.

Part of our joint agreements was that we would be open with each other and also tell each other if we wished to change something in our agreements. Aamod assured me that he still kept to our agreements, though he in fact had already broken them. This continued back and forth for two years.

The consequence of this was that we grew further and further away from each other and we felt less and less joy in life. There was a new distance and emptiness between us. I felt extremely exhausted and tired of trying to support Aamod in maintaining his openness and inviting me into his life.

It also created a deep confusion and sense of being lost, because I didn't understand why things weren't as open between us anymore. Despite this, I trusted Aamod's word more than my inner feeling.

Aamod: I had started abusing again in secret and lied about it. I was afraid that the abuse would be discovered and Sophelia would leave me, even though she always said that if any of my old addictions should return, we would help each other, seek external support and support each other in healing. She assumed unconditional love in her relationship with me. I didn't think it was possible that someone could love me unconditionally, as I still assumed my fear controlled my intellect and still carried a strong self-contempt and self-hatred. The consequences of my choices were that I slowly strangled contact with my surroundings and with my heart.

The fear, shame and guilt because I had violated the agreements caused me to choose to lie and try to hide the abuse and break these patterns all by myself. I couldn't manage this on my own, and fell back into old patterns and relapsed during these years. During this time I continued to manipulate myself and my surroundings and abused Sophelia's trust in me. My Air element/my intellect was in great imbalance; it dominated and had taken over a large part of my life again. The whole family was affected negatively by my imbalances.

Sophelia: My great sorrow and pain in all of this was that I trusted Aamod more than my own inner voice and truth, and in this manner I betrayed myself deeply. It was something that would take me a long time to heal (I felt that healing was possible only after our AuraTransformation™).

One day I read in the newspaper about AuraTransformation™ and I decided right away that I wanted to do an AuraTransformation™. Aamod didn't understand fully what it meant, but felt this was a very important step for the whole family. Aamod had trust, and we decided to do an AuraTransformation™ in November of 2013. Our son, who was born in 1994, decided to come with the two of us and do a so-called Aura Adjustment at the same time.

The more I read the book "Balance on All Levels with the Crystal and Indigo Energies" by Anni Sennov, the more hope and clarity grew within me. A deeper understanding emerged in why I chose to respond to the children in a way that other adults around didn't always understand, but which became increasingly clear to me the more I read and learned about the New Time childen and energies. I was completely ready for this energy shift and looked forward to it enormously.

Right after we made the decision to do the AuraTransformation™, which was two weeks before we did the treatment itself, Aamod could no longer hold back his lies and everything came up to the surface. This created a very deep physical, mental, emotional and spiritual cleansing for both of us. I was deeply shocked that I had betrayed my inner truth, my inner voice, and that Aamod had broken our joint agreements. I could, despite all of the pain, sorrow and confusion, land deep inside myself and my own process. Amidst all of this, I felt great trust for the treatment and the future. I felt that this treatment came as a great opportunity and gift for me, our relationship and our whole family.

However, I didn't know at this point if I wanted to continue in the relationship with Aamod. If it was even possible to build trust between us again. I was absolutely sure that I never wanted to betray myself ever again in my life. I decided to heal and to trust my inner voice and what I felt within me, as well as to seek support to heal. I didn't know if I wanted to invite Aamod into my healing process or if I needed to do it on my own.

We decided, despite everything, to travel together with my son and do our AuraTransformation™. The treatment was a very strong and positive experience for all three of us. We felt that we healed deeply on a whole new level. We stood as brand new before ourselves and each other.

Aamod: After that followed a period of emotional purging

and turbulence. I made a clear inner decision that I wanted to remain in the relationship, no matter what, even though Sophelia didn't know if she wanted to or could invite me deep into her heart again. For me, it became clear that I wanted to be with and live with Sophelia entirely on all levels.

That which had not been possible previously, was released under our AuraTransformation™, and our negative energy ties were cut, the co-dependency became more visible and repressed energy was freed. A whole new world opened up for us, and the change was a fact. This created a huge relief and hope that it could actually be possible for both of us to support each other in a mutual healing. The fear had turned into excitement and curiosity. We learned to walk again, step by step. To slowly get to know and start to meet each other again, in an entirely new dimension.

The illusion and the "fog" that I had lived in all of my life was released. I could see and understand on a clearer level how reality looked beyond the illusion. It was only after my AuraTransformation™ that I could see the destructivity in the choices I made on a deeper level. I could even see the extent and consequences of what my choices had meant for the whole family. How it affected our lives in so many different ways.

I felt that I was in touch with my inner truth, stripped down to the skin. It felt like I, for the first time, could see Sophelia in her whole being. Sophelia felt she was fully present in her own energy.

We felt the protection of our Crystal auras and we could begin to communicate in a new way and in several dimensions. Especially on the energy level and the consciousness level. It was both a shock and extremely liberating to experience that we were now two individual and closed energy systems.

A very intensive crystallization process and cleanse happened during the first six months in a more powerful way then we ever could have imagined. Our entire relationship and our family were transformed. We were thrilled for the opportunity we had received. Sophelia would never have dared to go further if there hadn't been such a large and permanent change in both of us. The whole family came into a much better balance, and all of the children/young adults found that I was much more enjoyable and easier to be with. I also experienced that I could see and communicate in a new way with the children where I could understand them more clearly than before. Sophelia felt she had energetically arrived home and could now, without obstacles, rise up in the energy tower/frequency, both on her own and together with the children.

Nothing could be left over from the past, everything had to come up to the surface and be cleansed in order to be clarified and heal. In the first six months while the crystallization process was most intensive, life went upside down for us. Sophelia still didn't know whether she would be able to build up trust in me again and want to stay in the relationship. That which partly made it possible for us to continue the relationship was my new grounding and my firm decision that I wanted to heal together with Sophelia. I could now take more responsibility because I was in my body. In the past I had often moved out of my body when it felt too heavy and painful to stay in it. Instead I now had the possibility to meet and receive my innermost self and be able to go through and heal. I was in touch with my feelings and my truth.

I created new patterns where I made sure not to become self-absorbed and to only see my own process and pain, but also to provide Sophelia with the space and understanding for her continued development and healing. Sophelia became increasingly conscious of what she needed to be able to heal and what requirements she had to ask of me in order to open her heart again. She stood by this. I became conscious of the responsibility I needed to take for my part in creating a balanced energy exchange in our relationship. This was one of the greatest gifts I have received in my life, as I alone haven't previously been able to set boundaries and break my negative/destructive patterns and take full responsibility for my well-being and my life. Now as the fire burned in my heart, I had more contact with my truth and couldn't lie or go against myself, which is a liberation.

The most positive aspect of our process was that the healing and the change were permanent. It was crucial that Sophelia chose to remain in the relationship.

A new sense of balance and joy began to appear for all of us.

We created new individual and joint agreements in our relationship. This was a necessity for both of us and for Sophelia to have time and space and feel safer in order to heal and build up trust again. We focused on creating new creative patterns that brought us forward, upward, and closer to each other. We were no longer stuck in our past.

Aamod & Sophelia: We increased our awareness of our relationship during the time we went through this change. We also made sure to get outside support and did recurring Balancing sessions where we both felt safe. We experienced on many different levels how our soul relationship was cleansed and transformed into a Spirit Mates relationship.

We had a feeling that this experience was important to us, so that we would be able to support other couples who are ready to transform their relationship to the New Time energy and new levels.

Our shared desire now started to grow stronger and clearer. We felt an emptiness in some areas of our lives for a time after the AuraTransformation™. We longed for something more!

We became conscious that it was our Dharma, our life mission that we longed to develop and manifest in different forms. A strong sense of creating a new togetherness grew and we now had a lot more access to our consciousness, our fire and our driving force in our lives.

We began to open ourselves to our life mission and how we could work together, and this driving force grows stronger all the time.

This whole process was such a positive development and experience for us that we decided to train to be Aura Mediators to provide this opportunity to other people and whole families.

In August of 2014, we attended the Aura Mediator Course together. To have the opportunity to do the training at the same time gave us support and an understanding of each other's process. It brought us even closer together. We each worked with our own energy and development, and we felt that our hearts and source expanded even more after the training. We both felt great joy working with AuraTransformation™ and the positive development it brought with it both for us and others.

We started at an early stage to give double Balancing sessions where we sit together and work with the balance energy. We felt how we began communicating intuitively with each other during the treatments with the client's energy. There it became apparent to us that our consciousness fused together in spite of the fact that we are two individual sources.

Aamod: Almost a year after the Aura Mediator Course we

went together to see Anni Sennov in Denmark and we did individual sessions with her and had our auras compressed. These sessions further boosted our creativity and we saw people's energy even more clearly, both through photography and when we did the AuraTransformations and Balancing sessions. We also found the understanding that it is part of our shared Dharma to highlight the beauty in people in many different ways and on many different levels. I had been working as a photographer for 20 years, but now we wanted to work together. We began to create images together in a completely new way, where the images grow before our eyes. We discovered how we complement each other in creation and how the New Time energy and people's individual energy become visible in our pictures. Our different qualities, as the tools we are, create and add a wholeness that we previously didn't have access to.

Our consciousness and our energy began to communicate more broadly, not just in higher or lower frequency, because we once again had come in contact with more of our consciousness.

Now it became even more important than ever for us to create balance on all levels. We had very little interest in creating or maintaining drama, neither in our relationship nor together with other people. We had a great focus on creating balance in the exchanges in our relationship, our personal energies, between our elements and between masculine and feminine energies. We were even more conscious that we needed to be careful with sorting energy both from the surroundings and between us. It was important for us to be able to maintain and build on our personal energy.

Aamod & Sophelia: The intimacy between us continues to deepen and we communicate energetically in a totally new way, beyond the intellect and the words. There arises a deep calm and unconditional love. We both feel deep trust in each other's energy and can relax and heal together. We support each other and feel great gratitude and joy for each other. It is rare for us to misunderstand each other and we treat each other with courtesy and respect.

When we are present together egos receive very little attention and the heart and the body receive a lot of nutrition.

We communicate easily and we often see and experience people and situations similarly, but we also have different perspectives and experiences. We can feel what is happening in the other's life, such as when the other is at work or traveling, without losing our own focus. It is easier to let each other go when we need to, and become more effective in our own personal energy and what we want to achieve in the course of the day. Prior to our AuraTransformation™ we were energetically entangled in each other and we could influence each other unconsciously, which wasn't always stimulating for us. Now we can support and inspire each other on the basis of a clearer position in ourselves, now that we are on our own individual energy systems. It was linked to a fear of being our own individuals before our AuraTransformation™, but now it is a feeling of freedom.

Time passes and we continue to crystallize and develop our relationship in even more dimensions. When we work together we are open tools for the source. We have discovered that our shared work has changed and become clearer and cleaner as the source leads. This is expressed by, among other things, the many shared projects that we have. We both work within healthcare as nurses, but wish to create a life where we can work together more with our shared Dharma, our life mission. We already travel a lot in Sweden, and increasingly in Europe, where we work with AuraTransformation™ and photography.

This Spirit Mates book is also a shared project where we contribute and work together with our story and photograph Spirit Mates couples.

Before we met we had both longed for each other for a long time. We remained in ourselves and continued to develop, and we both created different conditions for meeting. It took several years. We both needed to mature and develop greater consciousness in order to meet each other. If the meeting had taken place at an earlier stage we might not have managed to receive the development that we were thrown into when our hearts met. In order to speed up the process of finding your Spirit Mate, we believe that it is important that you take care of yourself and your energy in the best possible way and make sure you develop as a human being on all levels. The larger the balance you are in, the greater the possibility of finding your Spirit Mate and that your roads cross physically.

When it comes to the response from our surroundings concerning our relationship, it has varied. For us it feels natural to have a close and intense relationship where we exchange a lot of energy with each other. We love to be together.

Some have chosen to be inspired and others to be provoked. Some have thought that we are too "strong" together. Others have been curious and surprised by our relationship.

Many feel seen and safe with us, both when we work professionally and socialize privately.

Our children have always thought our relationship was positive and we are their role models. They often say that we inspire them to dare to believe in openness, respect, development and love in a relationship.

We are passionate about inspiring others to create functional, respectful and loving relationships, both in couple relationships and in family relationships. We have extensive experience in developing and healing dysfunctional relationships and co-dependency. And we ourselves have experienced that it is fully possible to transform these wounds/energy charges to create new patterns and creative/functional relationships. We feel deep gratitude to be Spirit Mates and to be a part of the New Time development of creative couple relationships.

Have you already met your Spirit Mate?

This story tells us just how important timing is. You can wish to meet your one and only Spirit Mate, but it can be a lot of work if you meet each other "too early."

After having an AuraTransformation™, it's obviously easier to get in balance on your own than having to deal with the imbalances of both parties in both your energy systems at the same time.

When reading Sophelia and Aamod's love story, it is clear to everybody that initially they were not in balance. They met each other at soul level, and on their way towards spirit level they went through a whole lot of challenges to achieve trust in their relationship before achieving trust in themselves, which is actually the opposite way of doing things compared to what most Spirit Mates couples do.

When looking from the outside, it seemed like Sophelia had already gone all the way from soul level to spirit level, and that she had worked a lot with personal development. It also seemed like she had learned how to be in balance and balance herself at a higher spiritual level, while Aamod had more to learn. However, Sophelia also had more to learn, because she didn't trust herself and her own intuition completely. She actually trusted her love partner more than she trusted herself.

Just because you have already met your one and only Spirit Mate and you are living together with the other half of you, it doesn't necessarily prevent you from having such challenging experiences in the relationship as Sophelia and Aamod did. This is because if you don't trust yourself, then both of you will continue to be hidden behind your respective "soul masks" where you are not able to see and show your true inner power and full spiritual love potential to each other, until the day when both of you see, trust, respect and love yourselves fully.

When expanding your consciousness from soul level to spirit level **you must trust yourself completely**, which is a very important step consciousness-wise. If, at soul level, you trust other people more than you trust your own spirit, you can easily be fooled or become a victim of their basic human needs for getting physical and mental satisfaction without having that same satisfaction by discovering it yourself. You suddenly become blind because you trust an energy that is out of balance and is not as pure as your own energy, and in the process you give your power away to others.

Your full spiritual potential can only be shown to your Spirit Mate when both of you have succeeded in passing through the veil of forgetfulness, where earthly people don't remember who they really are at spirit level. So, if you are one of the lucky ones who has already met your Spirit Mate and you both have full confidence in yourself and each other, this book is guaranteed to confirm everything about your amazing love relationship.

Then you know by heart that living together with your Spirit Mate is the most life-affirming experience of all, beyond even that of bringing a child into the world. You know intuitively, and instinctively, that meeting your Spirit Mate is a very important step on the path to bringing everything in life back to its source. And you also know that the Universe needs to bring together all Spirit Mates who originally grew out of the same cell division, so that the overall level of spiritual consciousness in the cosmos and on Planet Earth can be raised extraordinarily over the coming decades.

If you would like to learn more about this very specific topic, please read Anni's book "Golden Age, Golden Earth," which goes into much more detail than we will here.

Meeting your Spirit Mate is actually the fastest way to integrate pure spiritual love energy into your personal consciousness, so that you cannot help but love yourself, and consequently also love your Spirit Mate. Everything suddenly becomes so easy and simple, when two spirits who, at the very beginning of time were made for each other in an identical spiritual image, meet each other in the physical world.

So, as you can probably understand from reading this book, nothing in a Spirit Mates relationship can ever be compared to what most of us are accustomed to from previous relationships at soul level.

Karin and Anders

Love Story # 3

When did you meet?

We met for the first time in September of 2012. We had spoken for about half a year and gotten to know each other by phone. The first time we spoke as friends, as we both were in relationships. Then Anders' relationship ended and it didn't take long before Karin's also ended. We had become very curious about each other and fell in love without even having met. Meeting in real life felt very urgent and that meeting was powerful from the very first moment.

How did you meet?

We were both in an NLP (Neuro-Linguistic Programming) coaching course at the same school and Karin was in the year ahead of Anders so we didn't meet during the course. Karin was then living in Gothenburg and Anders in Tumba, south of Stockholm. Anders had the possibility during training to have Karin as a "luxury coach," i.e., to receive free coaching by someone who has already made progress in the training. Karin, as a luxury coach, got a practice client which was needed for receiving a diploma and certification as a coach. At first the intention was that Karin should have another practice client but he, conveniently, was never heard from. Therefore, Anders became the practice client.

Since we lived so far from each other, the coaching was done by phone. This was in February of 2012. These three phone calls were a high point for Anders. He looked forward to the next call and felt empty when we ended the call.

Karin had read Anni and Carsten Sennov's first book about Spirit Mates and knew as soon as that first call that Anders was her Spirit Mate and the man she had been waiting for.

Partly because they were alike in many ways – he was a male version of her in the way that he had also dared to try new things, changed jobs often, moved around in Sweden and the world, had several long relationships – and partly because he was very different from her in how he was brought up. He came from a true "Bullerby Village upbringing," i.e., very confident with stable family relationships, animals, farming and so on. Karin's upbringing had been troublesome and left many spiritual wounds, and she had realized after her previous relationship that she needed a safe, stable partner.

Was it love at first sight or when did you know?

Yes, it was love even before first sight because we got to know each other and fall in love with each other over the phone. When we met in real life the first time (in a hotel lobby in Borås) we could have probably gotten married then and there. Anders' heart almost jumped out of his body when he finally saw the fantastic woman he had unconsciously searched for his entire life. And there she stood, with a smile that must have lit up not only the hotel lobby but the whole city. Anders' eyes fill with tears of gratitude as he writes about this first meeting. Karin felt the same. It was wonderful to see his warm smile and when we hugged we didn't seem to want to let go.

How did you know that this was different and/or how did you become aware of it?

We both felt that this was a "match" that we had always looked for in relationships but had never found. Like finding the other puzzle piece, the male/female equivalent of yourself. Like finally, at last, feeling "complete." It was like an old cliché for both of us, something that we had never experienced before but that now had become a reality.

It's so obvious that we are better together than apart. The

feeling that 1 + 1 = 3 is made permanent with us. Sometimes it seems that 1 + 1 can equal 4, 5, 6 or even more.

How did you know that you were Spirit Mates?

Karin was already familiar with the concept of Spirit Mates during the first call with Anders (on the phone) and knew immediately that Anders was "the one" she had been waiting for. Partly through things he said, but also by the warm feeling and a kind of recognition.

Anders said to his sisters when he went to meet Karin the first time: "Now I'm going to meet the mother of my children," so he also knew somehow. Anders also read the book about Spirit Mates and understood afterwards what it meant.

Anders: Everything is complete on all levels. I have the experience of living with another person who knows me better than I know myself. Karin ALWAYS wants what is best for me. Sometimes I myself don't understand what is best for me and on those occasions I have the support and security with Karin. Karin is really my best friend and life companion. She is my best everything.

What has happened in your lives since you met?

Everything went very fast and it was very dramatic around us for a while. Anders' relationship had ended during the late summer, but Karin had a little more of a difficult time breaking up from her relationship – for several reasons. They had a child together and she knew that the breakup would radically shake up her world.

After not speaking for a number of months after the coaching, we began to speak on the phone again at the end of August – as friends – but soon enough we were speaking several times a day and our feelings couldn't be held back. Karin thought, at the beginning of these calls, that if she was going to break up from her relationship within six months, she should take it easy out of respect for her partner and the father of her child. This time was subsequently shortened and after just two weeks of calls she couldn't do anything else but end her relationship, and in the middle of September we met for the first time.

The second time we met, three weeks later, Anders proposed and Karin said yes. This was in the midst of the chaos that took place after Karin's breakup from her relationship, but it couldn't be stopped. There were incredibly strong feelings in circulation: anger and hatred mixed with the strongest of loves.

In the beginning of November Anders visited Karin and arranged a new job. Anders broke away from his life in Tumba and moved down to Tjörn, where Karin was now living. This was in December – three months after their first meeting.

After a few months we bought a house together where we later got married, just over a year after our first meeting. A few months more and we had our son Filip.

The chaos after Karin's breakup calmed down after six months and today we are all good friends and have a modern family constellation that works exceptionally well. That we work so well together with the older boy's father is thanks to Karin.

Tell us about some events and experiences from real life that you've had together so that people can get a feeling for how it is to live together as Spirit Mates

We experience a total reciprocity in our feelings. Even if we go through difficulties and challenges, there is always a basic sense of belonging together. Breaking up isn't an option, which it has been in the past for both of us.

It is quite natural for us to make decisions that "benefit the whole," not just one of us but what is best for both of us or the whole family. We help each other in all situations. They aren't "your" and "my" chores, but things that need to be done regardless of who does them. This means quickly managing things to then have time together afterwards. This can mean sitting and talking an entire evening on the sofa, as well as being close, snuggling or doing something fun.

There are never any discussions between us about who should pick up the children at daycare/after school care or who should change diapers; we are completely freed from that. There is no power struggle between us, no prestige in one or the other. There is no one that can "win" – how can you win over yourself?

Another example from the time before the beginning of our relationship: Before we met and were still speaking as friends, Anders thought about testing out internet dating. Karin, who had previously been both controlling and jealous, urged Anders to try this because she was so completely convinced that it would be the two of them later on regardless. Anders found a woman on the internet and made a date. When the day of the date was approaching, Anders canceled as it was not the right person. He had already made contact with his other half.

We have great respect for each other's expertise and great joy in each other's successes. It is like being happy with your own successes but even better; you can share them with your life partner.

What is so special about your relationship that you haven't experienced in any previous relationship?

We are each other's absolute best friend. At the same time we have a strong passion and also match each other on the mental, sexual and sensual plane like never before. There is a mutual understanding and support for each other's needs in all situations. A willingness to compromise is distinct. Of course we both have good and less good sides. It feels so natural to focus on all of each other's good sides.

When we are apart from each other we want to make the time apart as short as possible. It's physically painful to be separated. We live on an island and it is physically hard when we are on opposite sides of the bridge. It becomes peaceful when our other half is back on the island. We can often feel when the other has come across the bridge to the same side. We feel it in our whole body.

How have the people around you reacted to your relationship?

Everything went very fast; from engagement, moving, marriage and children, but for many it has been as natural as it was for us. They have been able to see that we have finally "hit home." Many people see us as role models for how a relationship should be. They see how we want the best for each other, how we respect and listen to each other.

Others feel threatened or provoked, find fault and try unknowingly to come between us. Sometimes it feels as if others watch and expect that things can't be as good as they seem because everything happened so very fast seen from the outside. Some people seem to have only been waiting for it to end, but are probably starting to realize at this point that it isn't going to happen.

Our engagement wasn't so official that we advertised it. For us it was for real, of course, but for others it was mostly just that Karin had a ring from Anders. In that Karin was already pregnant and people knew it, the marriage itself was no great surprise to our surroundings. It was mostly a natural step on the way. We already felt as one and were very happy to feel one with our name also. Anders changed his last name and took Karin's, which meant that the whole family now has the same last name, which feels really good. Hand on heart, we have never bothered ourselves with what other people think, and this is so natural for us.

Are you working together on a project or do you have separate work lives?

We already work together in a business besides our current "day jobs" and we want to work together even more, preferably all the time. We don't like being apart for long periods of time. We are better together as a whole. We have started a shared business and before we started we thought about what name we should use together. When we thought of the name Andrins, everything fell into place. Part Anders, "And" and part Karin, "rin." For us, it feels absolutely right; working together for real and, of course, with a shared name. In our business we work with AuraTransformation™, lectures/ training programs in health, NLP and coaching. We use each other as sounding boards in our different areas in things large and small. This can apply to pricing, type of work, lecture layout etc.

Had you already done an AuraTransformation™ or did you do it after you met, and if so, how has this changed your relationship?

Karin did her AuraTransformation™ (AT) at the beginning of 2012. Once we started our relationship, we were careful and wanted both of us to have the same energy, so Anders did his AuraTransformation™ shortly after we met the first time. A calm appeared right after we both did our AT. The calmness reached a new level after we both trained as Aura Mediators. The need to be close to each other and share large and small is always increasing. With AuraTransformation™, a new outlook on life begins that feels very important to be able to share. This makes our relationship even stronger.

Do you have the same interests?

We share many interests, such as the family, outdoor life, spirituality and personal development. We met through one of them; NLP coaching. But above all, we have shared values and can talk about everything. In fact, we only have a few interests that don't interest the other person. Even if one of us isn't interested, that person is always careful to encourage the other one to pursue their dreams and do things that make them feel good.

We are also always interested in discovering ways to deepen our relationship.

Do you have any suggestions or advice to give others who want to find their Spirit Mate?

Karin: I feel that many people who know about Spirit Mates want to meet their Spirit Mate immediately. I did too. But before I was aware of the term, I had had a dream that was very clear to me: Someone laid cards (like tarot cards, but with ordinary playing cards) and up first was the jack of hearts and later the king of hearts. The person laying the cards then said: "See, the jack of hearts comes there!" But I saw the king further on and said: "But I don't want to have the jack, I want the king!" Then the seer said: "But you can't have the king if you don't have the knight first." Meaning this: I would never have been able to understand and appreciate a man like Anders without the experience with the "jack" first. I believe that we need to have some experiences in order to see what truly is important. So dare to date, even if you don't know right away if they are "right," they may well be right at that moment in many ways.

Anders had thought that a small neat, dark-skinned girl would suit him and Karin wanted to preferably have a man who was taller than her, without a beard and maybe with another dialect. It didn't quite turn out that way as Karin is 185 cm (over 6 feet) tall and a strawberry blond. Anders is 177 cm (almost 5' 10") with a beard and from Småland like Karin. So, we have a similar dialect which isn't what Karin had in her idealized image. All of this has been totally unimportant to us as EVERYTHING else really is 100% right.

So a couple of tips are to skip the long list of "must haves" for your future partner. Try instead to feel how it should feel to be in the relationship, and find the right feeling. All the things you have written down on paper that would be ideal in a relationship and what is on the outside are irrelevant. Instead look forward to being amazed at all the criteria you didn't even know you needed that pops up when the feeling is right.

That we are Spirit Mates doesn't mean that we always think alike. On the other hand, it means that we always want to reach each other, which means that our attitude towards each other is always positive and solution-focused.

How to prepare for meeting your Spirit Mate

According to Karin and Anders' love story, it was clear to Karin right from the beginning that Anders was her Spirit Mate and that he was like a male version of her. This is because Spirit Mates are like two pieces of a puzzle fitting perfectly together, making them each feel whole.

When they combine their energies, the energy pool they now share expands greatly, so that 1 and 1 becomes 3 or more, and the effect of their united energy capacity allows the love couple to solve even bigger tasks and challenges than if each of them was alone. Because of the extended energy capacity when together, they can manage to do more things than would be possible if they were a Soul Mates couple.

After Karin and Anders connected on the telephone the very first time, everything started to go extremely fast in their lives, even though Karin tried to make a plan for when to leave her previous partner. Once the spiritual fusion process between her and Anders started, it wasn't possible to stop it, and Karin had to change her divorce plans and accept that everything was going to go much faster than she had originally planned. This is how things usually develop when two spirits recognize themselves in another body. Then the Spirit Mates Integration Process speeds up all by itself.

Like all other Spirit Mates love couples, Karin and Anders are each other's best friends and act as role models for other couples. They only had to compromise on their respective expectations they had for each other before they met. So now their best advice to those who have not yet met their Spirit Mate in real life, is to skip the long list of things they want from their Spirit Mate when they finally meet, because no matter what, they end up getting everything they want without really knowing what they want.

As Karin says, she could never understand and appreciate a man like Anders without the experience with the "knight." She thinks that we all need to get some experience from being with others to better understand what is important to us in our Spirit Mates relationship. So dare to date even if you don't know if the person is "right," because he/she may be right for you at that specific time.

Most people have certain expectations and wishes for how their Spirit Mate should be and look and where they come from, just like Karin and Anders had. If, however, these expectations don't match reality, they can actually keep the "energy door" shut to your Spirit Mate, who might be located behind the door. Then you won't be able to see each other due to different expectations and wishes for your future life together. Therefore, you should try not to be too picky or selective when you start searching for your Spirit Mate, because it may not benefit you in your quest.

For what happens if you are looking for a blond person, and for some reason your Spirit Mate has a different hair color when you meet for the very first time? Then you will miss a unique opportunity to connect with your Spirit Mate at an earlier time, because you are looking for the appearance instead of feeling the energy. This will most likely delay your energy fusion significantly.

So honestly, what is holding you back from meeting your one and only true love partner, who is the only person that fully reflects your own personality and spiritual potential?

Is it yourself, or is it because the timing isn't right?

What is holding you back from meeting your own energy in another body with a totally different background and life experience? Could it be that you are afraid of forever being dependent on the deep intense love that you will feel when being together with your Spirit Mate, or are you afraid of one day losing this intense and deep love that you have for each other, where it's better to not have been in love at all? Or does your existing love partner and other potential partners function as sorts of watchdogs so you can't get near your true love partner?

Where are you in your own spiritual process and how can you prepare yourself for meeting your one and only Spirit Mate?

As you already know from reading Sophelia and Aamod's love story (# 2), you must have confidence and trust in yourself to be able to set personal boundaries in your life, and to live a balanced life with your Spirit Mate. Besides this, there are several other things you can do to prepare yourself for meeting and living together with your Spirit Mate. In general, it's all about personal development involving your body, mind and spirit, and your personal behavior.

In the next chapter, you will find examples of how to prepare to meet your Spirit Mate and attract him/her as a love partner on a physical level.

How to attract your Spirit Mate

First of all, you have to know yourself; otherwise you don't know what to look for. Secondly, you need to work on your personal balance.

Here are some of the steps you must take in preparing to meet your Spirit Mate, who is another version of you in another body. Always keep that in mind.

Spiritual steps

- Start listening to yourself and to what your spirit wants to tell you.

- Expand your consciousness and get to know yourself even better on a spiritual level.

- Practice yoga and other relaxing activities that will help your spirit to get full access to your body.

- Get an AuraTransformation™, which will balance you on a spiritual level.
  Visit **www.auratransformation.com** for more information.

- Get one or more Balancing sessions from time to time after having an AuraTransformation™.

- Learn how to use our Energy Self-Defense tools and mantras to defend and protect your personal energy. Read more under *Physical and mental steps* on the following page. Visit **www.energyselfdefense.com** for more information.

- Learn about the four elements that we all consist of: Fire, Water, Earth, and Air, and get to know your own element combination. Then start to integrate and activate as much as you can of the different elements in a balanced and spiritual way.
  Visit **www.fourelementprofile.com** for more information.

Physical and mental steps

- Work on getting balance in your physical life. Have an extra look at your work-life balance and situation as these will especially influence your love relationship in a negative way if you are too busy or too stressed. The "love door" will stay closed when there is no balance around you.
  Visit **www.fourelementprofile.com** for more information.

- Learn how to use our Energy Self-Defense tools and mantras to defend and protect your personal energy, and to keep other people's energies away from you so you can stay calm and balanced. It's important to have a good mental balance if you want to be able to attract the right love partner. Otherwise, there may be a lot of stress, drama and manipulation in your love life, because your thoughts are all over the place and not where they should be: in your mind.
  Visit **www.energyselfdefense.com** for more information.

- Go to the gym or do another type of physical activity to create a good connection with your physical body so you can better understand your body's signals.

- Spend time in nature, where you can stimulate both your body and mind by walking, relaxing and emptying your mind all at once.

Behavior

- Work on changing your behavior to be able to get and stay in balance all day. For most people, there is usually a lot of work to do with this.
Visit **www.fourelementprofile.com** for more information.

- Spend time with other Spirit Mates couples. It can help start the process of you meeting your Spirit Mate and will make your energy system recognize and remember what to search for in your own Spirit Mate. The stronger power the Spirit Mates couples you meet have, the stronger the impact of their energies will be on your life and your personal energy.

- Prepare and make yourself ready to meet your Spirit Mate by learning and trying new things that you have always wanted to do or would not usually do, and by getting outside of your comfort zone.

- When you start believing that your Spirit Mate, the other spiritual part of you, is out there somewhere, it creates hope in you, so you will radiate love and happiness, which will help you to attract your Spirit Mate. The more positive energy you radiate, the easier it will be for your Spirit Mate to catch you on their "love radar."

When you have followed the recommended steps above, it doesn't end here. There is always more you can do to prepare yourself for meeting your Spirit Mate. That's the reason why we have created a big universe online, consisting of online courses within the four areas: "The Spirit Mates Universe," "The Energy Self-Defense Universe," "The four element profile™ Universe," and "The AuraTransformation™ Universe" where we also focus on the Golden Energy.

Visit **www.sennovpartnersacademy.com** for more information about our four universes online, and all our online courses. More online courses will be added continuously, so be sure to check the site regularly for new courses.

It's important that you continue to expand your consciousness at more and new levels until you get the feeling that now you have done all you can to prepare for meeting your Spirit Mate. Then hopefully, your Spirit Mate has done the same in his/her life, so you can finally meet.

It's up to both of you to make yourselves ready before you meet as a love couple, so there will be less things to adjust when you finally connect with each other in real life. The more personal development work you have done in advance, the more amazing the Spirit Mates Integration Process will be in your relationship. However, it doesn't work in the way that if you meditate a lot, then you should meditate even more to achieve a higher balance in yourself before you meet. Instead, you must be more nuanced in your personality and behavior, and open your mind to the diversities that are waiting for you in your future Spirit Mates relationship. So focus on developing more areas of yourself, and sample and try out new things that you would usually not be open to.

You and your Spirit Mate are copies of each other in spirit, not in physical life where you are supposed to support and learn from each other.

You cannot change another person, because they have their own free will, but you can motivate them to change by showing them the way, and in a way this is what happens between Spirit Mates, but is still different. You and your Spirit Mate are directly connected by an invisible thread, where you attract each other and impact each other by your respective actions, since you are spiritually connected. By making yourself ready to meet soon, you will most naturally impact and influence your other half on a spiritual level to also make themselves ready. It means that every time you take a step forward, the other half of you, your Spirit Mate, will feel a need to do the same, unless they are already there and have impacted you to take the step that you just took!

Now take the next personal development step. You can compare it to walking up the stairs towards a new plateau, where you are going to meet your Spirit Mate while being connected by an invisible spiritual band.

The numbers of steps are individual, because it depends on how much development you have done previously and how big your joint Spirit Mates dharma is. The larger the task, the readier you must be, and the more personal development work you must do beforehand.

It's also important to know that you should not rush through these personal development steps, because your Spirit Mate should also have time to follow you through your invisible connection, and your Spirit Mate might be in a different life situation than you. Maybe he/she is in a relationship, so the person may not be searching for their other half like you. The closer the person is to themselves and being their true self, the stronger they will feel that there is something wrong where they are, but we all know that it can take time to accept deep inside that what you are doing now may not be the right thing for you in the long run. So don't move too "far away" from your Spirit Mate by running up the development stairs, because then you risk that he/she cannot feel you as strong as before, because you are suddenly further away from each other energy-wise.

You most certainly don't want to stay alone at the right plateau for a very long time, but that's the risk if you get temporarily disconnected from your Spirit Mate because you are in too big of a hurry. So you must be patient.

Whether you should run up the stairs or you should choose a slower pace, is something you should sense and decide deep inside yourself, either on a spiritual level or in your physical body where you can always connect to your Spirit Mate, even before you have met as physical beings.

As you will understand by reading the 10 real-life love stories in our book, there are no two ways to prepare that are the same and work in the same way when you should prepare to meet your Spirit Mate. However, when you feel ready to meet your Spirit Mate and you think you have done everything you can to prepare yourself for the meeting, you should for sure send out a clear signal to your Spirit Mate, or even call on him/her, which you can read about in the chapter *The path to your Spirit Mate.*

What happens when you meet, and you are not yet ready

You can actually meet when one or both of you are not really ready to meet yet, and then you can't see each other even though you may be standing close to each other. Or, you notice each other right away if you are meant to be a couple at that time. Normally this happens when your joint dharma can no longer wait to be fulfilled.

If you notice each other but are not fully ready to unite your respective energies, the initial Spirit Mates Integration Process will start anyway, and you will eventually get together and start a love relationship. However, it will be a different and complicated process, since there will be lots of turmoil in the relationship, because of all the personal development work that each of you need to do to get into balance. Instead of you each doing your personal development work separately, it will now happen together with your Spirit Mate; so everything will be with a much bigger power and higher energy, since it will happen while having access to your joint energy capacity.

At the same time, you are going through the Spirit Mates Integration Process, which is a big task in itself, and where many things are going on. Now, all of a sudden, much more is going on in the relationship and these extra things are unbalanced, so everything can really get out of control in your relationship. This is why you should work hard to get in balance on all levels before you meet your Spirit Mate.

A Consciousness Mate can give you some really hardcore eye-openers that your Spirit Mate would never do, and a Consciousness Mate doesn't fit into your life as a perfect love match, because they are not able to adapt to your personal wishes and needs that are different from their own. What they can do is to lead you one big step closer to the real deal – to your one and only Spirit Mate. So when you meet your Spirit Mate and he/she seems to behave like a Consciousness Mate, life can be really frustrating.

However, once everything is settled in your Spirit Mates relationship, your Spirit Mate will love and appreciate you for everything you are, and for what you have accomplished and learned about yourself and life before you met each other. Therefore, you should maintain a positive attitude, and trust in life even if your Spirit Mates relationship doesn't feel like a dance on roses when you first meet. There most certainly is a reason for this, and often it has something to do with the activation of your common dharma.

You could end up splitting up because you are not yet ready for the big Spirit Mates fusion with your other half, but then you will for sure meet at a later point in time, when the timing is even more right.

If you are not at the same energy level when you first meet due to having very different backgrounds, it will usually take some time to get there and/or to decide where you should meet energy-wise. This is not something that you would actually discuss, but it's more that you cannot avoid making a common decision because it will create the foundation for your future life together. However, time will normally show where it's best for you to stay with your couple energy at a certain time, and maybe you will change your common energy level often. It all depends on your dharma.

If you decide to stay on different energy levels due to your respective work situations, cultures, etc., you will have to split up your energies very often to be able to function in very different spheres work-wise, family-wise, energy-wise, etc., and not many Spirit Mates are willing to accept that when they first meet. They want to unite and merge their energies fully, which can make the whole integration process complicated if there are many external circumstances to take into consideration, and that don't match each other so well.

A Spirit Mates couple can also meet when one of them is at spirit level and the other is on soul level. This will be the case if for example one part has had an AuraTransformation™ and the other has not, and then the same circumstances apply as if the couple came from two very different cultural backgrounds.

When a love couple is not aligned energy-wise, they tend to be more influenced by other people than by each other, and so they must sort their respective energies more often as a result. So, there is nothing wrong with being in different places with your energies in your relationship. You just have to take a lot of extra daily precautions to balance and protect your own energy from being influenced by your love partner and others in a way that doesn't match your own energy.

It's also not a problem to meet your Spirit Mate even if you don't speak the same language. As long as you know that you belong together and have a deep feeling of interconnectedness in spirit, then there is always help to get from various translation programs on the Internet, and you can also create your own sign language. Meeting each other under such circumstances will for sure create the opportunity of getting to know each other in a different way than most other love couples.

There are many love couples out there who are Spirit Mates without knowing it, because they have met at soul level. They love each other deeply and would never question their mutual love, and they live their lives according to whatever terms they have agreed to before they were born. So being a Spirit Mates couple has nothing to do with having an AuraTransformation™. However, having an AuraTransformation™ will make it easier for you to feel and know if you are Spirit Mates, because the new upgraded aura structure and energy system that you get from having an AuraTransformation™ will connect your spirit and body energy, so you can get direct access to your own spirit.

The combination of having direct access to your own spirit energy through your body, and meeting and/or living together with your Spirit Mate in daily life, is a life confirming experience that will raise the overall quality of your life to a much higher level than was possible at soul level. Then being together with your Spirit Mate will be even more attractive than "just" connecting with your Soul Mate, even if it ends up being one and the same person.

It's not the person that makes the big difference. It's the energy frequency that you get access to together with your Spirit Mate that makes life much more interesting than it was before. Bigger power leads to more and bigger experiences in everyday life, and that is what most people search for.

It's very important not to try to interpret and understand the things that go on in your Spirit Mates relationship in the same way you would do in a soul-based relationship. All New Time relationships are based on new premises and not on the old terms. So, if you mistakenly believe that your Spirit Mate does not love you, you are about to follow the wrong love guide. It's for sure not the updated and modern Spirit Mates Manual you are consulting. When consulting *"The Spirit Mates Manual"* that we have made as an online course, you will learn that you should always look at things in your Spirit Mates relationship from a positive angle, even if you have a bad day.

You know that things are not right if you or your love partner often gets jealous, because when love and honesty are fully present in your relationship, there is no room for jealousy.

Jealousy is the body's way of signaling that a person is unsure if the couple is going to stay together forever and that the person is afraid of losing their partner. Behind the scenes, on a spiritual level, this is a clear sign that you are not an ultimate love match.

Spirit Mates are supposed to connect with and embrace their other half, who is in another body, and they always know that the intentions of their love partner are the exact same as their own intentions. Therefore, it feels totally wrong to be jealous and to be intimate with others if it's not a part of a learning process on soul level.

With an open heart – and not a widely open heart that invites everybody in – there is no risk that you will ever allow yourself to be involved in a love relationship at spirit level that doesn't fulfill your inner needs.

If the couple for some reason has to separate their energies, it will feel totally wrong in their bodies. They will feel as if their bodies are about to be torn apart and it becomes very difficult for them to live. If, however, they agree to separate for a longer period, it doesn't necessarily affect their bodies in a negative way.

It's not possible for you to close the door by mistake when your Spirit Mate finally shows up, because when the timing is right, there is nothing you can do as a human to prevent love from getting into your life. All you can do is surrender to the love and try to find the best possible solution for how to make things balance in your everyday life with your new love partner.

Your Spirit Mate has lived in a parallel or opposite universe to yours until the day you meet, which is why you haven't been able to see and sense him/her before. You must be ready for love, and your love partner has to be ready for love too, at the same time.

Spirit love is an all-embracing energy with no strings attached, and your Spirit Mate always expresses the same energies as you in a way you can't resist. That is where the physical attraction comes in and raises your mutual love to a divine level that cannot be measured in any way.

Annelie and Jörgen

Love Story # 4

After almost 13 years together it still feels warm and tingly inside when we think of each other. We want to be close to each other, have bodily contact, and sleep close together, and this feeling and the love is mutual. We can both feel the interconnectedness between us, the feeling of being Spirit Mates and its power. We are each other's best friend and lover.

We have now lived together for a number of years, but it feels like we just arrived at the beginning of our life journey together. We don't need each other, but we want to be together and we choose to be together. Here comes the story of us, Jörgen and Annelie. About how we met and a bit about our lives together so far which, during the time of this writing, is more than 12 years.

Even if we, since the first time we met and still today, feel that we really belong together on a deeper level, our journey has been marked by many both amazing experiences and, of course, huge trials. It all began when we met for the first time on January 24, 2005. Annelie had then lived alone with her two daughters for a few years and worked as a hairdresser when Jörgen made an appointment for a haircut. Jörgen had, unlike Annelie who had lived together with the children's father for 18 years, no serious intentions in any of the relationships he had started. Our past love lives and relationships couldn't be more different. Annelie had no thoughts or plans for the moment of starting a serious relationship. Jörgen, however, felt for the first time in his life: "I began to have a desire or a longing for a serious relationship. I wanted more than what the previously sporadic relationships had been able to give me."

Annelie pretty soon felt, or rather, felt as soon as we met that:

"This is someone who will remain in my life; that I would like to have in my life." Right then I didn't really understand how, but thought it might be as a friend – a male friend to have fun with, as a completely platonic friendship. For Jörgen the feeling was totally different:

"When I came in and sat down in the hairdresser's chair, the situation felt surreal, in a very positive way. Wow, I want her; here was my dream woman in every way. But right then she seemed unattainable to me..."

We kept in touch, talked on the phone and chatted occasionally. A few hairdresser visits later we went out to dinner together. We talked, talked and talked. Jörgen managed to "miss" the bus home and taking a taxi four miles felt unnecessary. We agreed that he would stay the night in town, and he tried to get close a few times, but it wasn't time yet...

A few months later, we began to see each other more often. We were both searching for closeness and neither of us had previously experienced being close to someone in this way. There was a new dimension in our shared presence which neither of us has experienced before. It felt like we were in our own shared bubble, shared the same aura, and the whole body became calm and peaceful. We could sit close together, hold each other, close, close and just be. This feeling and the experience wasn't the slightest bit sexual; it was simply a calm closeness, a presence together. That the closeness also strengthened our intimate moments, was a completely new experience for both of us. It felt as though we fused together and became one. It was enormously empty without this closeness. We both knew that when we weren't together some part of the whole was missing. Deeper feelings began to emerge even for Annelie. For Jörgen this meant: "An amazing feeling to know that my feelings were beginning to be reciprocated."

Annelie: "For me, it was definitely not love at first sight. He was definitely not how I saw the ideal man of my dreams." For Jörgen, it was just the opposite.

One day as summer was approaching, we realized in our separate ways that it would either be us for real, or we needed to end what we had started to build up. Somehow we already knew that this was necessary, and both of us had made the same decision. No words were needed; we both knew what we wanted, and from that day it has been us. From having seen each other only now and then, we now spent twelve vacation days together, around the clock, with children and daily life. It felt like we had already lived together a very, very long time. Everything felt right. It now became clear to both of us that when we had stopped thinking or hunting for a partner, and only let the love come to us, then we found each other.

During our first year together we experienced a great deal of resistance towards us and our relationship. Disapproval and resistance from many different directions, in an unreasonable and strange way. We talked a lot about how it felt, that there really was an outer and collective resistance against us, how incomprehensible that even sounded. This only strengthened us more and we grew even stronger together. It also meant that we had to make active choices about us, if and how we wanted to proceed together.

After three months together as a couple, we drove past a small church and Jörgen asks the question: "Would you like to get married...?"

The answer came instinctively: "Hell no, why would we do that, once was enough..." We looked at each other, both of us feeling very disappointed inside with that answer that "just jumped out." After that, it took more than 18 months before Jörgen worked up the courage and dared to propose: "An engagement and then a church wedding felt very important. I wanted to feel that Annelie really wanted to choose me and had equally strong feelings as mine. It would confirm my love and our love for each other. The feeling was that if she didn't want to take a step forward, it was a sign that maybe we weren't meant for each other. All or nothing, that's what it felt like."

"I knew he was thinking and wanting to propose, but I also understood why he dragged it out, why he didn't really dare; I could also feel that way after my blunt answer outside the church. I also knew that he was the one of us who needed to take the step, make his decision, without my 'help.' " For Jörgen, it was very important that an engagement also meant a wedding, which he carefully pointed out. Of course the answer was yes with the added: "I've been waiting a long time for you to ask!"

We chose rings and a month later we got engaged at Tiananmen Square in China, an amazing September day in 2007. We quickly noticed that we felt very similar in many contexts. Both values and basic principles, but also style and external attributes. However, during the first years it was clearly shown that we had very different ways of expressing ourselves and saying things. In the beginning this made it seem as if we meant very different things, but when we began to discuss and explain in more detail to each other, it turned out that we almost always meant exactly the same thing. We just expressed ourselves in very different ways.

We had completely different baggage with us in our backpacks, different experiences, lifestyles, childhoods and trauma which have also characterized us very differently. The differences were many: one of us came from an 18-year-long relationship, while the other had relationships that lasted

6 months at the longest. One is an only child, the other has siblings. We are the same age, but there are 15 years between our respective parents. Even so, we experienced, and still do, that we think and feel very similar in almost everything.

We decided, and even said in the early stages of our relationship, that we would be open and honest with each other, and talk when something feels wrong, as good communication is incredibly important. With such different baggage in our backpacks, what doesn't affect or damage one of us can be very hurtful to the other. It doesn't have to be right or wrong, but to be open and honest with each other erases any misunderstandings.

We got married on the anniversary of our engagement. We did it our own way, the way we wanted to have our wedding. We decided on the church that Annelie had looked at for most of her life because it is tremendously beautiful where it stands, on an elevation with nature close by and pink in color. By "chance" it lies in the countryside where Jörgen was raised and has many ties. The church was thus a given for both of us. When we decided that it was time for the wedding, all the planning flowed extremely well, and was simple and easy.

We both woke up on our wedding day with an incredible inner peace; it was very clear that we were in the right place together in life. We really enjoyed our own preparations. No nervousness, and only pure harmony and happiness.

The day and evening were absolutely amazing and we can still say today, with the benefit of hindsight, that "everything was perfect."

Now we lived as a married couple, but were still living apart. It wasn't yet the right time to move in together. Now "we" had a small apartment in the city center, as well as a townhouse on the outskirts of the city.

We planned to, when the kids moved out, renovate Annelie's townhouse, and make it into our shared home. But everything can quickly change. Annelie realized: "I would never want to move into someone else's finished home, so why would I think Jörgen would want to do it in mine...?"

He didn't really want to either; it would never be his home, and it was suddenly very clear that we needed to move. We were both very grateful that the situation had come up and that we were so united in our thoughts. We didn't know when, just that moving it would be. To start with a new and shared home now felt obvious to both of us. We were ready to sell and move right away, we just needed to find what we wanted. It could be right away, but it could also be in several years, we didn't know when yet. The most important thing was that it felt really right for all of us. We had made our decision.

The next step was to talk to the daughters. What did they want? Could they consider moving and would they accept living together as a family? Both said yes. One cheered and wanted to live in an apartment in the city center, the other in a large house where she could have an entire basement for herself. But what type of housing did we want?

House viewings were on the schedule, but gave no positive feelings. An ad for a "perfect" apartment appeared, but disappeared as fast as it was posted. The disappointment was enormous, we felt immediately that that was our home. Now we just had to find a solution. To confirm the feeling we visited acquaintances, who "accidentally" owned a similar apartment. Our visit really reaffirmed for both of us this is how we should live. This was a Monday night. On the walk home we structured how we would go about it. On Tuesday we wrote a note together about a possible home exchange. On Thursday we got in touch with the association's superintendent and asked for help putting up these notes as the gates were locked. Imagine the surprise when he answered that: "Such an apartment is for sale, the owner lives in Umeå, but is here cleaning right now..." Annelie got the name and address and rang the doorbell with a pounding heart, introduced herself and asked to come in and look. We could. We decided and made an immediate bid for the apartment. That same evening, while we were in the grocery store, the broker called back and announced that the seller accepted our bid, the apartment was ours. We wanted to sign the contract as quickly as possible.

We sold our respective properties, cleaned and planned. We renovated during our summer vacations. We had great fun together. The feeling of physically exerting oneself, doing the work together, creating our home and having a shared result, brought us even closer together. Despite the fact that we worked on the renovation at least 16 hours every day, it gave us energy. This whole process: making the decision, searching, finding, buying, renovating and moving, had a flow that felt completely magical. After the first night in our new place, it felt like we had "always lived together" and that it had been ages since we had double housing.

We found that we really succeeded in manifesting exactly what we wanted, exactly when we needed it.

We now had the hope that life would be a little calmer, we'd get to enjoy more of life, fight a little less, but how wrong we were!

The youngest daughter became seriously ill, resulting in hospitalization. She was a minor and it was required that one parent live in the ward together with her. Annelie put her company aside to be able to be at her child's side full time, without having something to want to return to. This was to provide greater opportunity for recovery. In hindsight, we couldn't have made a wiser choice.

In the following months we lived as if in a haze, everything that happened was surreal and we, but above all, Annelie, went into our own bubbles and did only what was necessary. "I thought I alone could help my child recover and therefore chose not to let Jörgen in our 'hell,' I thought I was sparing him, but couldn't have been more wrong." It all culminated at last one night when Annelie collapsed, totally exhausted, both physically and mentally, and realized that this couldn't be done alone. That night Jörgen asked to be let into "our" lives.

We humans often do things that we think "we must" do, that others can't get by without our help. It felt important to both of us to want to be involved and stay in our relationship for our own sake, not for the other person's sake, by working together to get through the crisis we found ourselves in. We released each other, to make our own choices. That night we both chose us and our relationship in an entirely new way. That night we became a stronger team and even the daughter's health situation improved. Jörgen observed: "I had been waiting to be let in and involved, so my decision was already made. I wanted to be involved and to not feel demands were being put on me, made it even easier."

Slowly but surely our life situation became less critical. In line with that, Annelie collapsed physically. Her body, which hadn't had rest during the more than nine months that had passed with keeping vigil, hospitalizations and constant readiness, could no longer cope when it didn't have to be on alert. It was like piercing a hole in an enormous balloon, and all the energy just disappeared. The one of us with lots of ideas, projects and things going on, now slept 16 hours a day and had a terrible pain that moved around in her body. Thus the roles at home became reversed. During this period we validated each other, learned to see each other with new eyes and helped each other move forward.

We searched for answers to what caused our child's illness and health, her way of being, acting and reacting and heard about something called Indigo Children. We googled and read about this and then hope began to grow. A few days later a timely invitation came for a lecture about Indigo Children, which we of course signed up for. The lecture and the day totally changed our lives, in many ways. After reading a book about Indigo and Crystal Children, even more pieces of the puzzle fell into place. A treatment form called AuraTransformation™ was talked about. A treatment that we both were attracted by, and it felt therefore natural to undergo.

The first occasion we were able to get away from home for two days for the first time in a little over a year, we went to Stockholm and did our AuraTransformations.

The closeness between us became more apparent after the treatment, both physically and mentally. It felt as if we were linked together in a deeper and clearer way, on another level. The love felt stronger and clearer between us, which we didn't think was possible before because it was already so huge, strong and secure. The body contact, closeness and even sexuality felt stronger, in a very positive way. We were also more observant of each other, both physically and mentally. Everything felt more and more clear. We heard, for the first time, the concept of Spirit Mates and read the book "Spirit Mates – The New Time Relationship" and then many pieces fell into place. There was just a calmness and safe observation, "yes, it's like this"; we now understand what happened relationally in our lives. We have chosen not to put so much focus on the fact that we are Spirit Mates, instead we felt HOW it feels to be together. What do we want? What do I want? What do you want? Why do we choose to live together? Do we need each other, or do we WANT to be together? What we know and feel is that we have an enormous shared sense of belonging. That love is felt in the whole body, all the time. Thinking too much, that is to say, using the intellectual "brain," instead of the body intelligence in the heart, can ruin a lot.

We also chose to not discuss the treatment and the effects for the first few months. When we sat down and were going to go through it together, it turned out that we both had the same sense of the most important thing that happened after the treatment, namely: **A large internal peace as well as internal security, which hadn't existed in the past.**

After the AuraTransformation™ the energy returned slowly but surely to both of us, particularly to Annelie, where even her bodily healing started, and her body took nutrition again. "I also started to see for myself how I had behaved towards myself all these years, how I had abused myself. It wasn't at all nice, quite the opposite, but at the same time very important and instructive." The Aura Mediator Course in 2012 was another push forward for both of us, and now our future life began to take shape, at least on the inside. At the time Annelie was on complete sick leave, and on "good" days she managed to walk around the house with our dogs. Body pain was constant, the body was totally "burned out" and exhausted, and the pain was classed as fibromyalgia. The verdict came from healthcare: "You will **never** be able to have a job again, get used to the idea of a life with constant pain."

The inner feeling for both of us was exactly the opposite, things would get better, only time was needed.

"I knew that everything I had gone through had a purpose, because the self-perceived experiences in life are more educational than all schools and trainings. I needed to now sum up my experiences, and begin to learn from my 'mistakes,' in order to be able to pass this on to others."

In the autumn of 2012 Annelie started, even if it feels like we do it as a couple, her own company. We work together and consider the company our shared baby. We import ionic toothbrushes and are Swedish distributors of these in our shared company, Soladey Sweden. We also operate the Balansbutiken (The Balance Shop), a web shop with products for both body and mind, products that make you feel good and are consistent with our values. The range includes many of the things within health that we used or use ourselves. Annelie also works as an Aura Mediator™; she receives clients for Aura-Transformations, Balancing sessions as well as doing different types of massage treatments. Our own experiences and lessons learned are an important part of the business. For several years we went to fairs with the company, as a fun and different way to have time together and, at the same time, market ourselves. Jörgen's part in the company is big, and even if it isn't visible externally it's still equally important. Without the collaboration we have had in this, we wouldn't have been able to lay the foundations as we have. Together we have, slowly but surely, built up a solid foundation. Annelie, who was very ill physically, had the opportunity to calmly heal. Our summations of her past behavior, in particular towards herself, provided the inspiration for a book "Våra älskade ungar – En spegling av oss vuxna" (Our beloved kids – a reflection of us adults) which was released at the end of 2014.

Life for us as a couple is different now and different from the one we have been accustomed to for years. Up until now we have lived with disasters, conflicts and always problem solved. To not have this chaos around us can sound great, but it can also cause problems. It will be new and unfamiliar, which if we aren't observant and aware, could instead lead to new, unnecessary conflicts in order to have what we are used to. We unconsciously search for what we are used to having around us, because that feels safe. We were both fully conscious of this and we discussed the problem many times. Annelie had at this point reached a very good balance, both physically and mentally. Her body worked well, the pain was largely a thing of the past, her energy was back, and she had had time for healing. It was now Jörgen's turn, now it was possible for him to start unpacking his baggage, his backpack. There hadn't been room for that earlier.

In our first eight years Jörgen was the one who had his feet on the ground, he was the one who was firm and safe and kept stability. When this was no longer needed to the same extent he lost his footing. He lost his role and didn't know what to do, how he should live or act any longer. The roles were suddenly reversed. A Crystal-Golden grandchild also came into our lives and stirred the pot.

During these earlier years Annelie had searched inwards, in herself, to find answers to her existential needs. What did she need to heal, feel good and function? She had taught herself to simply put words on emotions, events and experiences in order to understand, accept and learn. That requires a lot of self insight, as well as discipline. Through this, negative experiences, memories and events have been changed into something that today generates power and pleasure for both of us. There was a hope that Jörgen would unpack his baggage in the same way, but it was apparently time for us to change places. He had been the down-to-earth one for many years, and now he totally lost his footing. The more stable and balanced Annelie became, the more "he began to escape." Instead of addressing and talking about what happened in him, he chose to do what he had always done earlier in life, which was to escape reality and pretend that nothing was happening. He chose to reverse back into old patterns and behaviors. He backed up energetically also. The mentality "What I don't address, doesn't exist" returned. Life becomes difficult when the other partner is very intuitive, and feels and understands what is happening, so "I let my husband go on his own journey."

Our relationship has always felt very good and the love has always been very strong at every level, so these kinds of doubts about us as a couple have never existed. Nor have we ever lost desire and longing for/to each other. Despite this, energtically you can lose both yourself and each other, which we did. We needed to make a decision about the future because neither of us wanted to remain where we had now ended up.

Either we grow forward together, or we choose to go separate ways. It couldn't wait any longer.

With this Annelie had made her decision about the future. Now Jörgen also needed to make his own choice: "I lost my familiar position in life and fell back into old patterns and behaviors. I had no idea how I would move forward. I felt as if I was at a dead end, without my own power to move away from there. This led to a great uncertainty for me, my self-esteem sank, I lost power and my energy level fell. To ask for help has never been my strong suit, but I finally had to, for my own sake. I didn't want to lose everything that meant so much to me, that I want in my life. I did actually want to develop, I just didn't know how at the time. When Annelie put her finger on the problem, I came to the realization. I wanted us to develop further together."

2015 was a very painful, fantastic and interesting year for us. Jörgen got help to unpack his baggage, he understood things more and more, and slowly but surely he too landed on a new platform, more in himself. We realized that we can hurt each other even though we are Spirit Mates. We have different baggage with us in life and different ways to unpack this in order to free ourselves from the past that no longer needs to be packed. Based on ability, personality and past events we also react differently. Sometimes people do things that "with the benefit of hindsight" also affect others around them. Just because you are AuraTransformed or living with your Spirit Mate, it doesn't mean that you are perfect. However, this can facilitate being able to, in a balanced way, make use of your consciousness and together understand, learn, accept and then determine how to move forward, both together and separately. You need to, of course, address your own baggage, even if you may need to get help on the way. Life together with your Spirit Mate can be easier, but even more difficult. The more conscious you are, the more dimensions are involved in life, the more aspects there are to relate to in the relationship, which can be experienced differently. Things, behaviors and events always have an underlying cause. To dare to see these isn't always easy, but is incredibly developmental. It was easier before to take the fast route, judge and opt out. Now it's very simple and natural when you have the ability to live from heart and body intelligence. There is, however, a big difference in that it's very difficult, not to say impossible, to deliberately be mean towards each other. We both learned a lot and after a very challenging year we came back, in terms of our energy, to each other again and the love between us grew even more.

As we write about our shared journey through life, we are hit by the feeling that it feels like we have lived a very long life together. At the same time we realize that we have only just started our life together. We have gone through many different phases, all of which meant a lot to us. Some have been fantastically fun, while others would have been very nice to have avoided. What we have both learned from our "mistakes" and positive experiences, is that we wouldn't want to be without them, no matter how hard it has been during certain periods of our lives. It is extremely positive that we, together, can sum up events and even see what we have learned.

Together we find joy and love in daily life, which is extremely important. We look forward to our day-to-day collaboration and delight in most of what we do together. We collaborate incredibly well on all projects we do together, whether it's working, building, cleaning, writing or whatever we come up with.

A relationship isn't about choosing each other once and then it's "us." Our relationship is choosing each other every day and all the time.

After the AuraTransformation™ and in life with your Spirit Mate, when you have learned to use the heart and body's intelligence, it's simple to acquire the answers from that. Without the brain getting involved, the possibilities are so much easier to see. The whole body feels love, joy and ease when it's right. If you know what you want most, it's much easier to move forward together. That's exactly what it means for us: to have a shared power and a deep feeling that we belong together, that we want to be together, that we can imagine ourselves aging side by side. So far this feeling has only strengthened during our almost 13 years together. We both feel it very clearly throughout our bodies. Many times we know what the other is thinking, feeling and wanting without verbal communication.

So far it has never felt that we need to be away from each other to feel good. We have never felt that we need to rest from each other's company to recharge. Neither of us has felt this in previous relationships, where "me time" had been necessary. When we are apart, traveling, working or having fun, it still feels like we are together on an inner level.

We hope that more people can have the joy of finding their Spirit Mate and can enjoy the ease, love and joy that we have in our relationship. When you choose each other because you want to be together, not because you think you need each other. Where the love and the attraction are there every day, in daily life, all the time ♡ ♡ ♡

Stop thinking and let love come to you. Don't get caught up in thoughts and worrying about if the one you meet, your love, is your Spirit Mate or not. You may have to meet one or more people before your Spirit Mate comes into your life.

With Warmth & Love
Annelie & Jörgen

How is it to live together?

Usually there are certain issues in a Spirit Mates relationship that require extra attention from the love couple when they live together, but in Annelie and Jörgen's case there have been extremely many different ingredients present in the relationship right from the beginning that required their full attention. So when reading their love story, we are sure that you got a feeling of having heard almost everything there is to know about being a Spirit Mates couple.

However, Annelie and Jörgen's love story illustrates *their life* together as a Spirit Mates couple, and not the life of all other Spirit Mates love couples, but wow, really many things have been going on in their relationship and family that most Spirit Mates couples are never going to experience in a lifetime. We can therefore conclude that there is a very high energy pace present in their relationship, and that they have gone through many development steps while living together that most other Spirit Mates love couples would have gone through on their own before meeting each other.

You can read more about Annelie and Jörgen and the experiences and challenges they've had in their relationship, later in the book after love story # 6.

When reading all the amazing real-life Spirit Mates love stories that we share with you in our book, you will know that there is no room for "love demons" in a Spirit Mates love relationship. A Spirit Mates relationship is all about balancing and integrating the best qualities from each other as well as supporting and embracing each other at all levels. This is what true Spirit Mates love is all about while at the same time being attracted to each other on a physical level.

So, if you are Spirit Mates and there are love demons in your relationship, you can be sure that these demons will continue to show their ugly face as often as needed until the problems that are causing the demons to be around, are solved and you have balanced out your personal energies in your relationship, as well as in your everyday life.

If you continue to argue and it doesn't feel natural for you to support each other in a positive way, there must be a special reason why you have met each other at this point in time. Usually Spirit Mates will not meet until they are able to embrace each other's energies completely.

Just imagine how two cells/people knowing deep inside that they belong together but who have been kept apart for a very long time, obviously need to be close to each other a lot, because there is so much love between them. This is how it is to live together with your Spirit Mate, and not only in the beginning. The love between the couple is simply so strong that it is always radiated from them, so it's obvious to everybody around them that something special is going on energy-wise.

Only when there are other people around or important things to take care of, will they separate their energies and focus on something else. Otherwise, it feels like the most natural thing in the world for them to unite their energies at all levels, hold hands and stay close to each other without even saying a word. They can also talk a lot and share ideas and visions, and in that case, they will always complement each other in a positive way.

At the beginning of the relationship the two Spirit Mates will go through a thorough integration process where they start to integrate both their energies at all levels in their respective bodies as well as on a spiritual level. And since they have been apart for so long on a physical level, there is a big need for learning everything about each other, and the sooner the better.

The whole idea of splitting up as a love couple at the beginning of their respective lives, and of integrating each other's energies again and again in every new life, is actually to learn from each other, since this is a very fast way of getting insight into what the other part has learned from this life. You can say that a continuous Spirit Mates Integration Process is going on in the Spirit Mates relationship whether it's here in physical life or on the other side, and both parties are growing significantly on a spiritual level due to this integration process.

When the two Spirit Mates integrate energies from each other, a bigger process starts where each single cell starts to look for the same cell in the other body and "compare information." Each cell will then mirror each other, so bad experiences will be overwritten, since the body is very intelligent at cell level, knowing what to copy and what not to copy. In this way all experience that is stored in the cells will be cleansed through mirroring your Spirit Mate at cell level, because you will not both have experienced the same bad things in life, which is one of the main reasons why you come from different backgrounds in physical life.

But how is it to live together with your Spirit Mate in physical life and what can be expected of you in such a close and intense love relationship?

In the deep love relationship that a Spirit Mates relationship is, there are always streams open for sending and receiving love and intuitive impulses between the couple. The Spirit Mates' respective consciousnesses have, right from the start, been working diligently to melt into one common consciousness, and once this merger is complete, it is totally impossible for either of the Spirit Mates to even periodically close off the exchange of energy and love between each other.

So generally, the Spirit Mates love couple will always help each other because in that way they also help themselves. Not because they want to help themselves, but that will always be the result of helping their love partner.

You always feel the spiritual and physical presence of each other, but actually it's much easier for most people to understand this when saying that you always sense when your Spirit Mate is not around. The main difference however, is that neither of you focus on what is lacking in the relationship. Instead, you appreciate what you have.

You choose your own actions in your Spirit Mates relationship and how you want to spend your time with each other. There is no compulsion, pressure or stress coming from your love partner that forces you to do something that you don't like. Love is the overall foundation in any Spirit Mates relationship, and you usually represent the opposite energies in any situation when it comes to Masculine-Feminine and Feminine-Masculine energies, which can easily change from one situation to another.

Interconnectedness in the spirit

When a Spirit Mates couple meets for the first time and they start to sense that the person in front of them is different compared to other people they know and are related to, they will usually get a feeling of being related not just as possible love partners, but also as relatives because they are Spirit Family. One thing is certain, they feel deeply connected in an inexplicable way.

To meet your Spirit Mate, is actually the biggest confirmation you can get in life that you have found yourself and your life purpose.

Many people think that you will fall extremely in love and almost lose your mind when you finally meet your Spirit Mate and that everything is super romantic day and night. However, this doesn't always happen to be the case when you are finally together.

Everything is and feels exactly like it should and is perfect in all ways, even though you rarely know what it takes to make your life feel perfect. You maybe thought you knew what would make your life perfect before you met your Spirit Mate, but it is not until the day you meet your own energy in another body with completely different life experiences than yourself, that you know what is actually perfect for you.

In short, Spirit Mates surround themselves with an optimal energy of love, balance and cohesion, which is difficult to achieve with a partner where you do not have the same human and spiritual standpoint in life. So, if you do not feel that you can share all your thoughts and feelings with your current partner, it might not be your Spirit Mate.

If there are problems in a Spirit Mates relationship, this is always due to external events or persons. The love couple itself does not have an imbalance in their relationship, but old trauma and bad experiences from the past can easily find their way to the surface when they meet. Not because they trigger each other, but because the honesty and openness in the relationship can bring all imbalances to the surface so they can be balanced out. Therefore, it is recommended that you have cleared up all your own imbalances and unresolved things and issues in your life, from the period before you meet your Spirit Mate, so you are ready for the new relationship when he/she finally turns up in your life.

If you have already met your Spirit Mate without knowing it and without succeeding in your relationship, there are definitely still unresolved and/or unrecognized truths that you just have to get in place before you can get together. This can of course also apply to your Spirit Mate.

There are things from the past, which in the long term can be devastating to a loving Spirit Mates relationship, if they have not been balanced out before the parties meet. Therefore, it is so important that you do all you can, to balance your personal energy and expand your consciousness before you meet.

Most importantly, however, is to find out what your dharma and spiritual life purpose is, so you can begin to realize it before you meet. Then you, and the overall life force that we are all part of, don't risk that you suddenly forget to live your dharma because you'd rather kiss and be together with your beloved Spirit Mate all the time.

In fact, the biggest confirmation you can have regarding having found yourself and your life purpose, and that you have left your past behind you, is that you get the possibility of meeting your Spirit Mate and live a balanced life without fighting all the time. If you then meet resistance from people around you because of your new Spirit Mates love relationship, just let go of the resistance and let those who no longer can and will follow you in a positive spirit, feel free to disappear out of your life.

However, you need to be aware that before you meet your Spirit Mate, you will most likely have a mission on soul level in the old soul-ruled hierarchical system that you must remember to let go of when you meet your Spirit Mate. Otherwise, the soul mission is likely to follow you into your Spirit Mates relationship, unless you are so lucky that you already have completed the task before you meet.

If the soul mission comes along because you have not been aware of getting rid of it when you meet your Spirit Mate, then those who follow you and are supported by you at soul level, will get much more power at their disposal caused by your fusion with the energy of your Spirit Mate. Because when your personal energy merges with the energy of your Spirit Mate, your mutual energy capacity will more than double.

If you experience unnecessary resistance from the outside world in your Spirit Mates relationship, it may be because those you have previously supported, consciously or unconsciously, are unhappy because they no longer have access to your full attention and/or energy. And when they get extra energy from you on an unconscious level without knowing it, because now you also have access to your Spirit Mates' energy, the surroundings will unfortunately get extra power from you to create extra resistance towards you and your new love partner, which is a rather complicated situation to deal with.

If, however, you have released your soul task before meeting your Spirit Mate, then fortunately, such a situation will never occur.

Why should you choose
a Spirit Mates relationship
instead of a Soul Mates relationship?

Deep in their hearts most people have a need and a longing to love and to be loved.

If it had been possible to unite all Spirit Mates, on the physical level, right from the beginning when the soul energy was still in operation, then from a pure spiritual point of view the couple would not have been able to work constructively together in everyday life. There would have been a risk that due to their inevitable spiritual merging, the Spirit Mates would have stopped all human contact with the outside world, simply because they didn't need other people in their lives than their love partner, the other part of themselves.

This would not happen because they were egoistic and selfish, but simply due to the overwhelming experience it is for most people to meet themselves and their own energy in another person. Just imagine how it must feel to explore your own energy through somebody else's body and mind, which is what happens when Spirit Mates meet.

They would quite simply have been enough for each other and would have found it very difficult to let go of each other in daily life, which has never been a part of the overall plan for human development here on Earth.

The goal for uniting and merging the energies of Spirit Mates is not obsession, but unconditional love.

However, in the old soul-based world, spirit duality could easily turn into physical and personal obsession if any couple were to meet with its full consciousness potential, before being fully in balance themselves. This is the main reason why Spirit Mates have not previously had the possibility of meeting each other at a physical level in real life on this Earth.

Having a great power and not using the excess energy that comes from uniting the love couple's two energy pools into one big energy pool that can contribute to raise the overall energy of our planet and of humanity, would simply be a waste of good energy. So that's the main reason why Spirit Mates have a common dharma that they must focus on when they meet, so that meeting each other is not the main goal itself. The main goal is to activate and fulfill their common dharma, and getting the opportunity of uniting their two energy pools into one big energy will then be a gift of gratitude from the higher powers to confirm to the couple that they are on the right path in the physical world doing what they are expected to do.

In the old world, until around the year 2000 – when the soul energy was in control and love relationships were based on a consciousness attraction and balance between opposites – also called soul partnerships – Spirit Mates would have lost a part of themselves if they had surrendered completely to love and to each other. So, at soul level Spirit Mates would have been very jealous and obsessive towards their love partner, instead of providing space for true love in their relationship, simply because they didn't want to ever separate their energies from their spiritual love partner again, now that they had finally found each other in the physical world.

Unlike soul energy, spirit energy corresponds to a person's full consciousness potential. This energy allows space for a more flexible, comprehensive and holistic way of being, as well as a deep respect for each individual.

On the physical level, spirit energy concerns itself with the person's body and vigor as well as all the possible ways they can have of being able to express their energy.

On the spirit level, no consideration is given to the individual's old ways of thinking. Certain emotions, which could previously have made people act inappropriately in the company of others are not given consideration. With spirit energy, each and every individual is expected to have let go of all their old soul-based energies and ways of behaving, since at soul level people didn't mind letting any personal imbalances play out in relation to the whole.

Instead, it is expected that people will always seek an overall positive development for the benefit of the whole, while simultaneously preserving their own energy.

With soul energy, everything is predetermined down into detail, and all human thoughts and actions are completely attuned to the whole in order for the huge earthly and karmic jigsaw puzzle to move into a higher frequency based on balance and fairness. Spirit energy and Spirit Mates however, represent a free-flowing love energy which can seem highly unpredictable for many people.

In a Spirit Mates relationship bodily contact, touching and sex often have a very high priority. The "plug and socket" metaphor does apply, in both heterosexual, homosexual and transsexual relationships. With this plug-and-socket effect, Spirit Mates can and do accumulate a large amount of consciousness and bodily energy by bringing their bodies together as often as possible. As their consciousnesses are already united and therefore forever linked, bodily contact can only support this spiritual connectedness in the most beautiful way.

It is unconditional love that is expressed when the couple has sex, and that is why the dream of being with your one and only love partner suddenly takes on an even greater meaning. Infidelity is never an option when both parties have upgraded to the spirit energy and their consciousnesses are fused together. Why should you look for a partner who is not identical to your own energy and who doesn't mirror your energy in the exact way you want it? It will only cause trouble and drama in your relationship.

If you look at the Spirit Mates' individual physical and personal characteristics, you can see that they are often very similar to each other. They are not necessarily completely identical in appearance, but due to the equality of their energy, you could be led to believe that they might be related to each other, which, in a way, they are. Except that they are spiritually related rather than physically related.

In the sexual relationship, this similarity is often evident, as the couple are perfectly compatible in a bodily way and they have the desire to do the very same things for and with each other.

One of the Spirit Mates will bring energy from below thanks to their good earthly grounding, while the other will bring energy from above with their greater connection to the spiritual dimension. This will continue until the couple has exchanged so much energy that they can each get energy both from above and below. This leads to the possibility of an orgasm, which is both internal and external and cannot be described with mere words. It needs to be experienced.

So those are the options you can choose from when deciding whether you should choose a Spirit Mates relationship instead of a Soul Mates relationship. As you can probably understand from reading this, there is a lot more energy to be invested in a Spirit Mates love relationship than in a Soul Mates relationship.

A Spirit Mates love relationship is a total investment that lasts forever, while a Soul Mates relationship is a short-term investment, where you cannot be sure that you will be together forever and ever into eternity, which, however, is the result of being together with your Spirit Mate.

Once Spirit Mates are connected, they can never be separated again, because what is rightfully connected in spirit can never be separated by any human on Earth.

Are you willing to leave your existing partner and life for your Spirit Mate?

The next love story that is shared by Kajsa and Heine is so beautiful and touching, because there is so much love and respect for all involved parties in everything they do and have done, and in all that has happened between them before and after they realized that they were Spirit Mates.

But there has also been a lot of sorrow and emotional pain in their relationship which fortunately is not the case today, now that everything has settled between them as a love couple, as well as in their surroundings.

It can take a very long time for a Spirit Mates couple to get together, even if they are made for each other and come from the same spiritual source. The fact that others perceive them as a love couple, although they may not be a couple yet, and that the couple feel very comfortable in each other's company, doesn't make it easier for them to leave their existing partner and life behind, if they still love him/her very much.

Kajsa and Heine's love story confirms in every way that the unconditional love and total honesty between a Spirit Mates love couple can create the foundation for an optimal journey in daily life both as a love couple and as individuals. And when the love couple has sex with each other and unites on a physical level it always feels like a divine union where they get full access to the spiritual source through the intimate connection with each other's physical bodies.

The more they unite their energies as a love couple, the more attracted other people who need their help and support are to their energies. So the more they transform as a love couple on an inner spiritual level, the closer they get to their dharma as a couple and individuals.

Whether it was the opportunity of finally fulfilling their common dharma, or it was their mutual love for each other that finally brought them to live together on a daily basis, is difficult to determine. It was obviously very difficult for Kajsa to leave her existing life and relationship behind, because it was also based on love like her new Spirit Mates relationship with Heine. It was just another kind of love. So there were many important elements to take into account during the long period where Kajsa and Heine gradually got closer to each other both personally and spiritually.

Another important issue was the big age difference between them, because Heine is 14 years older than Kajsa, which may seem like a big problem when you look at things from the outside. However, if you ask any Spirit Mates couple that loves each other unconditionally, if it's really an issue and has a great impact on their daily life, they would usually say "no."

A big difference in age is not an issue in a Spirit Mates relationship and never will be. Only to the surroundings which will sometimes influence the couple's view on things and delay their spiritual fusion like it did with Kajsa and Heine.

As you probably understand, there can be many good reasons for not merging your energy with your Spirit Mate at first sight, which in some cases can turn it into a very long personal and spiritual journey for both parties.

Heine and Kajsa

Love Story # 5

Neither of us was looking for a new partner. Still we met. Maybe it was fortunate that neither of us knew it that evening in January 2009, the first time we met. Imagine if we had known that "just tonight you will meet a person who will make a total impression on you, and you are going to live with this person in four years." Had either of us dared to meet? Had either of us dared to meet the myriad of feelings? The deep friendship, unconditional love, grief and despair, frustration and doubts, the total joy mixed with even more doubt and resignation? The deep friendship and the love for each other drove forward and carried us carefully through the years of maturity, waiting for each other and then eventually uniting. When we met neither of us was ready for the other. We weren't yet ready for a life together. We lived in each of our marriages, with husband/wife and children. Neither of us was looking for a new partner; however, we were searching for ourselves.

We both had individually undergone a significant spiritual development over a longer period of several years. We had lived through difficult periods in life, and in our desire to be whole we had made a great effort to find peace and harmony in our separate lives. Several insights had landed in us and a greater love for ourselves had begun to flourish. Unaware of each other, we met ourselves on different levels. There were spiritual workshop evenings organized in the city where we live where different spiritual themes were explored and discussed. It was at one of these workshops that we met for the first time.

Kajsa: I was nervous on that first evening that I was going participate in, there was an electricity in the air that I couldn't put my finger on. I was going to challenge myself once again to see if my wings carried me.

I had worked for many years as an environmental engineer with different employers where technical issues were discussed on a daily basis. Spiritual questions had always been interesting but it was only after a deep depression at the beginning of the twenty-first century that I needed to meet myself to find a greater meaning in life and why I am here on Earth. The insights would, in time, lead me toward a greater balance and harmony, and personal development and spirituality thus had a very great importance. I lived in a marriage with a man I loved, together with our beloved little son. We had restored the house we lived in together and now we looked forward to enjoying life. My husband was understanding about my new spiritual priorities, but didn't share the interest himself.

When I walked into the room several people were already sitting there and I didn't know anyone at all. There were two people I immediately noticed, a man and a woman. The man had beautiful white hair and sharp blue eyes. It was also clear that he took good care of his body. Only much later was I to catch his name; Heine. The woman was the same age as me, a little mysterious and secretive beautiful woman with dark thick wavy hair. The woman, Maria, became with time a very close friend to both of us and one of the few people that would wholeheartedly support us in moments of doubt.

The workshops followed one after another without Heine and me even speaking to each other. I could now and then curiously wonder who Heine was, how he lived, where he worked, what his family looked like, what his wife was like etc. We had no real interest in each other and we weren't drawn to each other, but all that changed after our first conversation.

Heine: I had for many years been interested in the spiritual world and had read some books on the subject. I wanted to know more and borrowed books and spent free moments reading. I went to a meditation course which brought me deeper into the world I felt drawn to. I had undergone some difficult periods in my life, with grief that had deeply affected me, and I felt that I was losing more and more energy. I found it difficult to get through the days without sleeping several times a day. I loved to work out and with no extra energy for my workout I was starting to give up.

As if by accident I saw a small ad in a newspaper. "Healing" the ad said, and I gathered my courage and went to visit the man who later turned out to hold workshop evenings with spiritual themes. I felt immediately at home in this fantastic world and was not late signing up for the courses. There were about ten nice people signed up and I didn't notice anyone special – I thought. Afterwards, far later, I could describe Kajsa's hairstyle, clothes and how she moved when she came into the room.

Kajsa: It would take a year before Heine and I first spoke with each other. And once we started we couldn't stop. We felt immediately at home with each other and we could completely be ourselves. Heine is 14 years older than I am, has four adult children and was in a completely different stage in life during this time, but in spite of this we both experienced the discussions as free flowing and in deep unity. The age difference was just a number. We could laugh at anything and everything, and intuitively we knew what the other was feeling or thinking without asking. Very often one expressed what the other was thinking, and was unaware of this. It felt like the thought idea was our own. A close and very deep friendship began to develop between us and we both felt an immense joy, and an immense unconditional and pure love for each other.

I thought of Heine as a very close friend, the dearest friend I had, and our friendship was so natural that it couldn't be questioned. The deep love was so pure and natural that in connection with a dinner with friends, siblings and parents, I naively explained that I had a new friend whom I loved deeply. The comment wasn't appreciated by everyone. We both had a naive hope that our respective families would be able to socialize and be friends. I really wanted to meet Heine's wife and Heine was curious about who my husband was. When all was said and done, all four of us met at a barbecue at my home. But of course our respective partners weren't interested in socializing; actually the opposite. They probably felt our energies at an unconscious level and couldn't interpret what they were experiencing. Our energies were becoming more provocative and I, especially, was often met by comments and reprimands to stop my friendship with Heine.

During the time that followed, we went together to several different courses in personal development and explored esoteric concepts. Participants in all of the courses greeted us as if we were a couple, even though we were just very good friends. We took it all in calmly. At one point a woman corrected another and said: "They aren't a couple..." and the other woman said: "Oh yes, they just don't know it yet..."

After a while I discovered that I was pregnant again. A very eagerly awaited child was growing inside of me. I had a clear sense that there was a strong meaning with the new baby's creation, almost like a karma that wasn't yet finished between me and my husband. I would become more aware of what this karma was about some time later. Months went by and one starry night in April my second son was born. The joy and unconditional love that I felt the moment I held him knew no boundaries. While my husband and I were at the hospital Heine took care of my older son, who at the time was nearly four years old. Heine had taken care of him several times in the past and he was always overjoyed to be with Heine.

Sometime later, we were ready for the next step in personal development and together Heine and I did our respective Aura-Transformations. Six months after this, in January of 2012, we trained ourselves to be Aura Mediators. Sometime after our AuraTransformations we could both experience a greater unity between us with a feeling that our energies were searching for a unity. We longed for each other's company; just to be close to each other meant everything. In each other's company we felt uplifted, more energized, more creative in our thought flow and simply happy. It was like a dense fog dissipated in front of our eyes and we saw each other suddenly in a new light, which also created a lot of confusion. Should our friendship move on to something else? At this time, Heine had managed to divorce his wife, and for his part his love for me had deepened to a new level and life had turned into a long wait for me. I closed my eyes to this truth and didn't want to know, didn't want to take a stance.

Heine: Some days were completely chaotic. Sometimes I felt like I was going to collapse in my uncertainty about whether or not Kajsa would get divorced. It was clear to me that Kajsa was confused; she wanted to turn over every stone to find ways back to her husband and her marriage. If she didn't, she would rush into things and the consequences could be disastrous.

Time passed and the idea of consulting a reliable medium was born. We decided on a well-reputed medium. We contacted the same person, each at different times and for different reasons, and the answer for me was anything but uplifting. I also decided to only ask about general things in life and not ask questions about my relationship with Kajsa; I simply didn't dare.

The session took almost an hour and started coming to an end when the medium wondered if I was interested in hearing about future relationships. My stomach tied up and I heard my own voice as if it was in the distance saying: "Yeah..."

The answer from the medium came fast and strong! You have a relationship with a woman but it's nothing serious, just some sort of fleeting passion. You won't live with her. The passion will pass and disappear and a new woman will soon come into your life. She will be there for a short time, then another woman will come along. This woman will make the sun shine in your life and you will dance on rainbows... I felt destroyed. I had just heard the words I least of all in the whole Universe wanted to hear. My despair knew no boundaries, and just then at that moment my faith in life and the future was destroyed. I didn't want and I couldn't imagine living with someone other than Kajsa. How would I be able to do that? She felt like a part of me and how could I continue my life without my second half? I, who hadn't had any short relationships in my adult life, didn't understand why I suddenly would now, and two in a short time. I decided that the medium was wrong! She simply must have interpreted the information wrong.

One evening a few weeks later, I was struck by a thought. The idea was really more like a very sudden realization that just appeared. In my mind I saw the transformation, Kajsa's Aura-Transformation™. I saw Kajsa before the AuraTransformation™, when she found herself at soul level, I saw her in the short Indigo phase and I saw her after the AuraTransformation™ in a higher dimension. The medium was right, but still wrong! The three women the medium described were one and the same woman; Kajsa, described during the different phases of the AuraTransformation™, which the medium couldn't see or understand. My happiness knew no boundaries, and I was sincerely grateful for this absolutely invaluable insight. Now it felt like nothing could come between me and my beloved Kajsa. With that realization, we experienced liberation and relief, and a sense of truth grew stronger in us. We can almost describe it as the feeling of something big and true that came to us, but we didn't really know what it was all about.

Kajsa: My purpose in consulting the same medium was to ascertain the karma band I felt that I had with my husband and what it was based on. I had a strong feeling that, with the birth of our second son our collective karma was completed, but I wanted to get a deeper understanding of what it was all about. I was aware that the medium could have certain limitations in her ability to read the future because of my Aura-Transformation™. I was therefore determined not to ask questions about the present or future, just about past lives. I was indeed confirmed in my feeling that the karma was completed, as well as several other things that could be an explanation for how our marriage had developed. Heine came up, whereupon the medium convinced me to receive information about the future. The answer was equally disheartening as it was for Heine. Heine would never be anything more than a casual love affair but, she added frustrated: "You are stuck with one another in some odd sort of goo. I've never seen anything like it!" Much later, we were struck by the thought that the medium actually may have noticed our fusion, which certainly had already begun even though we didn't live together and hadn't had sex with each other.

Heine would have to wait for me for two years before I was done and ready to get divorced. We were both marked by these years with a lot of despair, confusion, doubt and resignation, but also with endless joy and deep friendship. Somehow we felt carried by our love for each other, which gently brought us forward regardless of mountain or valley. The discussions were numerous and lengthy. These two years were extremely difficult, but also a period of development in our lives. What gave us strength was when we both tried to turn our attention toward what felt true, permanent and genuine. We dreamt about a reunion between us where our respective families were friends.

We were familiar with the expression "Spirit Mate/twin flame" but we didn't know what it really meant. Our references were soul relationships with our soul mates, and it was these qualities that we both assumed regarding love relationships. Heine could, on some level, remember the original connection between us, but I couldn't. For my part, this resulted in the brain having more space than the heart and a kind of common sense dominated. I was determined to focus on my marriage, not in the least for the children's sake. In retrospect, I can understand that it really was the fear of the unknown, the fear of losing the children, the fear of regret and several other fears that guided my choices and my actions for a long time. It wasn't only my husband that I would separate from, but also from the children who were very small. An enormous sadness and a bottomless pit grew ever larger in me and somehow I felt that I was losing a part of myself. At the same time, deep inside me, there was a longing for Heine which sometimes spoke as pure physical pain in my body. This period of time was extremely stressful for all of us. My health was deteriorating and I often felt drained and empty of energy. Heine stood firm in his love for me while I was being torn in two emotionally. I eventually felt that I had to trust my own inner knowing, by overcoming the internal resistance which consisted mainly of my fears. Divorcing from my husband wasn't a solution but in the end it was the only option. The situation became untenable and the next phase had to take over.

After my divorce, life became totally chaotic but changed over time to where I had a great need for peace and quiet, to be alone and heal. Heine and I went through our divorce processes at completely different times and our needs looked very different. Heine had to some extent managed to land in his life on a new platform, while I and my children's healing had just begun. Heine wanted to immediately start a new life with me, but for me followed quite a long time of healing. After my divorce Heine and I saw each other basically every day and after about a year, we chose to live together. It would take almost two years for me to find my inner platform, reset my compass and no longer glance in the rearview mirror. We had to become complete as individuals, both on spiritual and physical levels, and in our separate ways, before being able to fuse into one. This process went on parallel to our daily life – while we cooked, played with the children, worked and studied, as well as loved each other. There was a deep sense the whole time that what we had together wasn't "just another soul relationship." Over time I could open up more for Heine and he got ever more space in my children's lives. The more we opened ourselves to each other, the more there was a feeling of a tremendously deep connectedness that we never experienced in previous relationships. The memory of our soul band became increasingly apparent to both of us as it was brought to life.

Heine has from the first moment had a close relationship with both of my sons and they have accepted him as an extra parent, a person they can turn to at any time, and it's clear that he is helping with security and love for their part. Heine's four children were all over 20 years old and were young adults. They lived their own lives, had their own finances and were independent. They accepted our relationship and could be happy to see their dad more happy and harmonious than they felt he had been for a long time. I received an even bigger family and more family members to care for and love. It made it easier for us, not in the least in view of the new transformative process that we eventually face more and more.

The moments with the experience of unconditional love

flowed ever more between us. But there were also moments of doubt; quite a few actually. We could both switch between hope and despair, that feeling that this will never work... There were even moments when I, with some fear, gave the age difference space. "Would Heine age much faster than me, and what would it mean for our relationship?" was one of the questions I asked within myself. It actually took two years for us to realize what everything was about. We both had a naive notion that everything would be so great between Spirit Mates, from the very beginning. It wasn't supposed to be such a roller-coaster with constant swings up and down as it had been for us. We didn't know we'd be thrown into an incredibly strong transformation process that mainly took off when we were physical the first time, our first sexual encounter with each other.

We mirrored ourselves in each other, all the time, every day. We mirrored our untransformed parts in each other, all of which haven't yet healed and transformed into a higher consciousness. Absolutely everything was forced to the surface to be transformed. Instead of allowing the process to run its course, we wanted to counter the process, among other things by projecting these energies towards each other, with the result that a stream of conflicts arose. We didn't know better! We used the ancient and inefficient tools we learned from past relationships, imprints from childhood and even from previous lives with the result that our transformations have taken longer. We both find that there isn't just this life that will be transformed, but many past lives will also be transformed and healed. Even past lives where we played different roles with each other. We both returned to old patterns that no longer served us as they once did. It was clear that all the old patterns, reactions, thoughts, imprints, memories, feelings, experiences... yes, *everything* that no longer served us would be transformed into a new vibration. It became increasingly clear that we were transformed into a new vibration that would match our individual vibrations but also our shared vibration, which still exists in the highest degree. We could see that every time we tried to project our unhealed parts of ourselves towards each other, it was ruthlessly clear that everything was about ourselves. We both felt equally strong the pain we caused each other in connection with these projections, and we were forced to find other ways to deal with the purges. Just the knowing and the insight of what everything was all about means that as soon as we see a mirror of each other, we take a step back and consider the energies that want to come forward. What was it that wanted to show its face? How could we meet it in the best way?

One of our best moments is when we meet in unconditional love and make love together – reunited in our shared original vibration. The experience is that everything is released and the energies flow freely between us. In moments of absolute climax we are brought together in a complete union and become one. We really become *one*, on all levels, and the reunification between us is extremely palpable. Our experience is that our energies dance with each other, love each other, merge into a single unit and in which our masculine and feminine energies become a single shared energy. In these moments we are not alone. It's quite clear that we are part of a greater whole where we are our own energies, but also in union with a source that is the origin of everything. It's simply totally unlike previous experiences from our past relationships. We live in a kind of shared Truth that our reunion is marked by every day. We feel that our unconditional love heals *everything* and there is nothing that is too difficult or too dark that can't be healed. It feels like we have chosen an almost totally developmental journey in this life. We also believe that this is part of what Spirit Mates are all about, to give us the greatest possible development depending on the individuals we are and depending on what we came here to do. This developmental trip probably looks totally different for all Spirit Mates. Some can certainly have an easier trip with few difficult challenges, while others may have to work pretty hard with their challenges. We think this is partly due to the individual's total consciousness, as well as to which degree the Spirit Mates will fuse and what the shared life mission is about.

Kajsa: Shortly after we moved in together our lives began to change more or less. For my part this meant that new opportunities became available. Suddenly it was as if the road was wide open to develop new knowledge, as well as manage skills that already existed and develop them further. A completely new knowing was taking shape, a knowing that actually already existed but wasn't expressed. As a child, it was natural for me to read the energies of all living creatures, people, animals, trees and other plants – yes, everything! I grew up surrounded by high mountains and influenced by Mother Earth's own energy. When I developed eczema as a teenager, I found healing through homeopathy, with the result that alternative healing forms became an interest early in life. Classical homeopathy was therefore a given and most obvious career choice when life suddenly offered new paths and development. My life mission suddenly became completely clear! Much of what I built up and established up until then, a nearly 20-year career as a civil engineer, crumbled and fell apart. Now I could instead manage my knowledge of energies of how we heal our bodies through energy, people and animals. I had my own experience of healing through homeopathy, and when we as Spirit Mates and family experienced that the new transformation process was stressful for our bodies and our minds, we found good support and healing through classic homeopathy, both for ourselves and the children. We also found good support through additional Balancing sessions when needed, and physical training of our bodies, preferably outside in our forests and mountains.

Suddenly I found myself in school again studying for a multi-year international education within classical homeopathy and medicine.

The knowledge of classical homeopathy has provided deep insights into how the body works on all levels, how we heal physically, mentally and emotionally, and become more whole as individuals and thus find spiritual peace. For both of us, for most of our lives, we have cared about our planet and how we achieve a kind of sustainability in our way of life, and this is in tune and in harmony with all living things. As a 20-year-old, I decided to study to become a civil engineer to work with environmental issues and be able to influence – at the very least – the environmental choices people made, and to purify what was once contaminated. I worked for one employer after another: consulting company, government agency, and local authorities, and over time, as the years went by, a new insight began to take shape. I was suddenly aware that we humans can only find spiritual peace when we heal ourselves and expand our consciousness. It's only then that we can cooperate with each other and all living things, including our planet, and to achieve a kind of sustainability. I was therefore forced to first look over my own life and clear away anything that didn't serve a higher purpose. But I reached a limit, and the doors to be able to work in a new way seemed to remain closed. This changed when our energies found each other. It was only when I was ready to work in a new way. With Heine's support and encouraging words everything became easier and even more pleasurable. Today, I run my own clinic in classical homeopathy and receive patients for treatment.

Heine: For many years I have felt like a powerful healer, with a very clean and clear energy which applies both in this life and in countless past lives. Throughout my adult life, I have worked in municipal operations as a caretaker and operating technician at sports facilities. For 40 years, I have met and supported a great deal of children and young people through my work. I have always found it easy to communicate and reach out to children and young people, and children of different ages always seem to have a natural attraction to me. I have somehow always chosen to operate in secret, even though I understand that I have a natural talent for visibility and openness and have no problem with giving of myself. For many years I lived in a beautiful and very old forest with my wife at the time and our four children, as well as a few goats, horses, pigs, dogs and cats. I lived close to and in harmony with nature, and it was there, surrounded by moss, lichen and creatures of the forest, I again found myself and my inner potential. During my hunting trips there were many long moments of silence and solitude with only the trees rustling or the water rippling as company. During these moments, there was ample time to sink into myself and just be in the moment. Many thoughts about Life itself and my place and importance on Earth were born during this time. I regained my ability to heal people and animals and I developed my ability to talk to animals. The old energetic forest gave support and unending love of my dormant abilities that now were brought to life. I became more sensitive and could feel the energies, and with time read these energies. I felt helped and strengthened by the healing I received for myself from a time when my body and my mind were too tired after some difficult heartaches. I could continue to explore and develop my abilities, but I also came to a point where I felt stuck.

We had both been living our lives with our feet on both the gas and brake pedals at the same time. When we were reunited, there was no turning back any more, there was no "cooling off period," and the brake pedal was removed. All we could do was to wander the way of the heart, although it was demanding. We both feel how we are constantly pushed forward at high speed and we are constantly presented challenges to solve. Thus, we have the opportunity to continue developing our individual potentials, and together these potentials are considerably more powerful, which becomes all the more obvious by the day. We feel that even this aspect is totally united with our reunion as Spirit Mates. We both feel an intoxicating joy and eagerness to be able to work based on our respective potentials and life missions, and the joy and desire to interact with each other is overwhelming. Our absolute experience is that from the moment we really chose each other in our hearts and accepted each other as Spirit Mates, we opened up a whole new reality that we could never have dreamed of.

Today, we work more and more side-by-side with our different tools within healing through energies. When asked for, we do AuraTransformations, as well as Balancing sessions individually, or as a team. We both have a genuine desire and drive to help people in their healing process in order to achieve spiritual peace. At the same time, we feel that this is just the start of something much bigger. The feeling is that we are maturing into the next level, and that over time we will work from another new vibration. Our respective lives have been characterized by constant development with new vibrational levels. But after our reunion, it meant that this whole process was accelerated to an unimaginable speed, and new paths have suddenly become completely open. We understand that the rest of our lives will be this way, where we continually reach new levels of vibrations in a way we hadn't been able to do individually. Life is truly magical!

The transformation and healing we have done together so far has resulted in a completely new perception of ourselves. We feel an ever more increasing genuine and deep love for ourselves, and with this, also for each other. The way we support and respect each other feels stronger in a way it didn't before our reunion. We allow and respect our individual energies and potentials, everything we are as energy beings, more and more. For us, the initial transformation as Spirit Mates exclusively focused on the love of ourselves, which showed itself in the form of cleansing and transformation of everything old that doesn't serve us anymore. We have now acquired new insights and a sense for what self love is really all about. The next step in the transformation process concerns an even deeper connection between our energies. It's quite clear that everything within us will be transformed and will vibrate in unison, for a higher purpose. It's a transformation that takes place in all areas of our daily life, in all the time we spend together, but also away from each other, and in our sexual union. Our experience is that we are heading toward a kind of overall energy. Increasingly, we understand that our sexual union involves every aspect of who we are, which is why this theme is worth mentioning again. It's not at all possible to compare with experiences from past relationships, even though we both have had good and beautiful experiences. The sexual attractiveness we experience is so much more than the sexual attraction we could experience with previous partners. It's as if a creative producing power grows and expands in a way neither of us has experienced. In our physical union, we take in more of each other's energies where we also fuse together in our energies. We feel, through our sexuality, that in these moments both transformation and integration occur in our energies at the same time, as it's a source of infinite pleasure and healing. In the heartfelt love we feel for one another, we can explore our sexuality in a safe and playful way. We feel our love as ever-flowing and where we allow each other to be just as we are. With the help of each other, we bring forth our highest potential. We simply bring out the best in each other!

As Spirit Mates, we know that we both carry the masculine and feminine energies, but for both of us our energies had remained in imbalance. We both have chosen to adapt to different life situations and, depending on who we are, we have chosen to integrate more or less of the energies. For Kajsa the masculine energy has had a larger space at the expense of the feminine, despite feminine energy being her true essence. Heine, on the other hand, chose to integrate more of the feminine energy, at the expense of the masculine which is his true essence. Therefore, we have both lived our lives based on an unbalanced energy platform. Since we have opened up for each other's energies in trust and love, Kajsa has with Heine's help found her way back to her feminine sexuality, which also turned out to serve as a portal to her feminine wisdom and power. Even Heine has, with Kajsa's help, opened up to his masculine wisdom and power through his masculine sexuality. Together we are now manifesting the masculine and feminine energies in a fine balance and harmony. Our experience is that we become clearer in our expression as individuals and a kind of acceptance for our true essence has emerged, who we in truth are – no more, no less. It has meant that the people we meet also accept us in a new way. People have namely, for quite a while, thought it hard to place us. During the years we were just friends, we were often seen as a couple. When we eventually became a couple, we were instead seen as relatives (which in some ways we actually are...)! Many times, our energies have also provoked and we have been met with resistance. A resistance that has come directly from individuals, but also from a subtle collective energy that was provoked by our energies. With our ever increasing clarity, people now rarely have any doubt about us, and misunderstandings and resistance are, thankfully, rare.

Our experience is that the more united we become, in ourselves as individuals but also as Spirit Mates, the more attractive we have become to people who value and need some of what we can contribute. In line with the inner transformation, the external reality has reflected the internal. We feel more and more every day that we have a larger role to play. For this to happen, many pieces of the puzzle have been forced to find their place, and there still remain a few more. We are maturing every day for something larger. We have understood that we will contribute to helping people in their processes, both on individual levels but also on a global level. Our mission is, among other things, to help people raise the physical body to new vibrations. For that to be able to happen, healing must happen – physically, mentally and emotionally. In this way we can help people to finally find spiritual peace. When people heal and find inner peace, this energy has a ripple effect. More and more people are affected by it and more people want more of that energy; that is our absolute conviction. We live in a time of change, and it's with the help of this energy that we can create more love in the world, and break down that which is destructive, outdated and no longer serves a purpose. We live in a time when it's becoming increasingly clear that everyone should live their life according to their true essence, and if we can, by being Spirit Mates, help in the process, we will more than gladly take on the mission.

To meet your Spirit Mate/twin flame is a journey in itself. We know from personal experience how transformative, challenging and wonderful it is. The love drives everything up to the surface to be healed, so that Spirit Mates will be able to live a life in harmony and total love. Without us being conscious of it, we prepared ourselves for each other through our individual development. We met at a time that many surely considered the least suitable and we can also agree with that. But on the other hand, maybe the timing couldn't have been better? We don't believe there is a best time in life for when it's suitable to meet your ultimate love partner. It happens when you are ready for it, no matter what life looks like. Once you finally meet your Spirit Mate the question is whether you are willing to make any changes necessary for a reunion to be able to take place. When you choose to live life with your

Spirit Mate, both responsibilities and commitments follow towards yourself and also towards your fellow human beings.

The higher meaning of being Spirit Mates is quite clear: to manage the shared energy and the potential in the best way and then to pass it on in the way intended, in clarity and with humility. What we get back, as a kind of reward, are endless opportunities to develop both as individuals and in our relationship. It also includes love for ourselves, our family, our fellow human beings, Mother Earth and all living things. We may meet the energy we in truth are, our essence, and we may meet it in reinforced form because the equivalent energy of ourselves can be found in our Spirit Mate. Our experience is that it's not possible to do anything halfway. It really is all or nothing and the good thing is that everything is done in balance!

Epilogue

Heine: The differences in living with Kajsa compared to my other relationships are multiple. When we first met we had inexhaustible topics to discuss. Our main interest was esoteric issues that neither of us was able to discuss with our former partners or most of our friends. There was simply no interest on their part. With each other, we found a tireless listener and a give and take of all sorts of ideas and thoughts. Kajsa is a very insightful and intelligent woman who reasons and discusses in a different way than I'm used to, compared with previous relationships. She has a very high consciousness and it's reflected in her reasoning in most things. When time now also includes our daily tasks, I find no one who listens with such interest and no one who gives me such inspiration as my beloved Kajsa.

I have, in my choice to live with Kajsa, undergone a great personal development, a development which will continue as long as I live. Kajsa has opened many doors in my life that I never knew existed. The door to the fantastic physical relationship we experience. The door to a richer inner life and, not in the least, the door to our fantastic Swedish nature. I had spent many hours in my forest before, hunting and fishing, but when Kajsa showed me her beloved mountains a whole new world opened up. She has taken me on fantastic mountain hikes in the Kiruna mountains in northernmost Sweden, which she knows as well as the back of her hand. Together we have experienced the most wonderful moments in this wilderness. We have given each other Balancing sessions sitting on a mountain slope with grazing reindeer as curious onlookers and with mountain streams humming in the background. We have witnessed our friend Maria, during one of our mountain hikes, giving a Balancing session to Kajsa's 75-year-old mother at the foot of Mt. Nallo, 900 meters above sea level. We have experienced the magic of the northern lights play of color in the shadow of jagged mountain peaks in a silence that can't be described.

My life has been enriched in a way I never thought I'd get to experience. My beloved Kajsa takes me on indescribable trips, both physically and spiritually, with a never ending joy and enthusiasm.

I would finally, with these sentences, like to declare my boundless love for Kajsa.

What a fantastic gift it is, to have united with my Spirit Mate in this life!

A gift is to lie next to her every night and always smell her special wonderful fragrance. A gift is to wake up at night and see her, to see beyond her physical form and see her original true essence, to feel it, to see it again. To recognize this essence through eons and at the same time to feel an indescribable joy produce fierce streams of joyful tears running down my cheeks.

The gift that is the greatest of them all is to wake up in the morning and feel my beloved close by and know that no one can suit me better... no one. My beloved Kajsa! ♡

Kajsa: To share our story wasn't a matter-of-course at first. We had many considerations, including if we wanted to get into and feel all the different emotions again that we experienced through the years when everything began before we became us. There was so much we felt – huge joy and confidence, and also a lot of suffering and pain. We also wanted to take into account our ex-partners who might read our story and we didn't want to cause them more pain than they had already gone through. I told my ex-husband of our intention to write our story and I felt that we can now start, now we can share our journey.

To live with your Spirit Mate/twin flame is both transformative and totally amazing and we have tried to describe our journey, our experience, as best we can. During the writing we discovered almost immediately that many new thoughts received new space and many new insights were allowed to grow to a wholeness and truth. We feel, thanks to the fact that we chose to open and show our relationship to the rest of the world, that we have taken our relationship to a whole new level. When I and my beloved Heine could start to live our lives together, it was far from self-evident that we were Spirit Mates. We were invited on a journey that was both shaky and uncertain, but we felt deep within us that our relationship would bring us both to a new horizon, to a completely new knowledge, if only we continued forward together. A knowledge that has actually always been within us and, thanks to each other's keys, we have accessed it. The most significant is the inner discovery of ourselves where love for ourselves opened up our love for each other and vice versa. We feel that we are completely free with each other, no disguises and no forced roles – a stable balance. We have landed in ourselves and in each other, and the feeling of having come home is highly apparent.

Heine's tireless support and encouragement for me personally meant that the insights around my own inner journey over the last four years have become clearer in a way I had never dreamt of. How I have known, without knowing, what my path and my purpose have been. It's like a wind blew away all my doubts and just left a place for the pure knowledge. My beloved Heine has given me the necessary space in life for this to be able to happen. Our personal and shared life purposes have come forward more and more; not forced but only in maturity. It's like when the insight is there, when it's made conscious, it no longer needs to be enhanced and defended, just lived. We experience a kind of simplicity in life. Working based on the platform we stand on is easy when focus and commitment is clear and not forced. We live out our truths and our life purposes more and more in balance, flow and constant synchronicity.

Our respective children follow in our life rhythm and together we have found a fine balance. Heine and his former wife broke off contact, perhaps because they don't have children together. When Heine and I chose each other, my ex-husband wished us good luck, which shows his greatness in spite of everything we have gone through. And it's clear that he also quickly found a new platform in life where he lives his life in greater flow, balance and love to himself. My former husband and I feel that we are better parents to our children thanks to the inner harmony which is present. We celebrate the children's birthdays together and it feels natural and straightforward. It wasn't so from the beginning after the divorce, but with time we have found a balance and harmony and we can all socialize as friends. It was as Heine and I hoped from the beginning, that we with our former partners would be able to spend time as friends, but neither of us could by any stretch of the imagination imagine that it would be like this. For my part there were more friends who broke off contact in connection with the divorce; not only with me but also with my former husband. In time, several new friends came into my life, beautiful people with very high consciousness and who have come to be very close friends.

In my eyes and in my heart Heine is absolutely the most beautiful and most loving person I can live with. I feel infinite joy that he has come to me and I am proud of myself that I finally had the courage to make the necessary changes to be able to continue our lives together.

Warm thanks to Anni and Carsten Sennov for giving us the opportunity to share our story! ♡

Our sincere wish is that we can encourage more to follow the heart's path regardless of the challenges along the way. Everything is possible – everything will be alright!

We wish for those of you reading our story, from the bottom of our hearts: Warmly, Good luck on your life journey! ♡

Your dream about the perfect family

For years Ewa-Lotta had a dream about meeting her one and only love partner and I, Anni, actually had the pleasure of meeting her when I held a course in Finland just a few days before she and Roger became a love couple. I remember that I saw her future husband being so close to her energy-wise when we left the course place, that she could almost touch him with her energy. Like he was standing just around the corner but still being unreachable to her as a love partner on a physical level.

Ewa-Lotta was in such a lucky position that she already knew deep inside who her Spirit Mate was and therefore they ended up getting married in less than two months after they moved together. There were no complications and no frustration, just a lot of things that had to be in place, so their future life could start. It was like everything had already been planned for years and was now ready on an energetic level to be acted out in physical life.

The stage curtain was about to be pulled aside for the big love adventure to take place in physical life, but the actors were not yet in place on the physical stage for the big theater play to start. However, when they entered the stage, everything went really fast at all levels in their lives.

Ewa-Lotta and Roger both wanted a family, so they got married, had two children within three years, and new chapters are added to their love story every day, because there are so many beautiful things in the pipeline for this happy Finnish-Swedish love couple and their children. They are the perfect example of an optimal Spirit Mates Integration Process where everything has been totally synchronized between them from the very first day they were together. This is usually the case when the family constellation or situation is a part of the couple's common dharma.

If your relationship is not like that and you want to learn how to balance between being a love couple and parents, and what you can do to better take care of your love relationship, we warmly recommend you to read Anni's book "Love, Sex and Attraction – A Short Guide to a Successful Relationship."

By relating to a number of key elements in a simple and realistic way, it becomes much easier for you as a couple to "create" the relationship you want. On top of that, you become much more aware of what is important to you in your relationship.

Roger and Ewa-Lotta

Love Story # 6

I, Ewa-Lotta, have had my highest and greatest dream for many years: That I would meet a partner, a man to share life with, who didn't have to be exactly the same as me, but that understood and appreciated me for the person I am.

I had previously lived in a highly destructive relationship, and after the breakup devoted a great deal of time to personal development by reading literature on healing and spirituality, and attended different courses and treatments, such as healing. I didn't want to, under any circumstances, enter into a similar relationship as the one I had just left behind me.

I made a great collage, a so-called treasure map, where I gathered pictures of the future that I wished for me. Then I hung that collage in my bedroom and looked at it every day, and thought that I already had everything I wanted, and in this way used the so-called law of attraction. I also wrote down all the characteristics I wanted my future husband to have. I put the list in an envelope which I then sealed and saved. I also used different affirmations with the purpose of attracting the man that I was supposed to meet. However, I was also aware and convinced that when the time is right we will meet, i.e., I didn't need to go out with light and lantern and look for him since at the right time our paths would meet anyways. I must admit that I sometimes found it difficult to believe that I would ever meet him, and it was sometimes as if I was on my way to give up hope, but on such occasions I tried to keep thinking positive.

During this period, Roger had been living in a relationship for many years. He says that the relationship had been in decline for a long time, but neither one had made a move to leave. Roger says that he had always hoped to meet the right person (but deliberately didn't search for her).

I, Ewa-Lotta, first heard about AuraTransformation™ in the summer of 2011 and I knew that this was something I had to do, no doubt about it. In August of 2011, I did my AuraTransformation™. And without going into more detail about how the process was afterwards, my life changed enormously.

When Anni & Carsten Sennov's book "Spirit Mates – The New Time Relationship" came out in 2012, I was quick to order it and read it very carefully from cover to cover several times! I even sent out the thought repeatedly as described in the book "Where are you my Spirit Mate? I am ready to meet you!" and continued to have faith that when the time was right, then our paths would cross.

During the late summer of 2013 it happened that my car needed to undergo a major service. I spoke about it with my girlfriend's husband who said that his friend, who has a garage in our town, would certainly be able to help me. I was pleased and asked him to talk to the guy named Roger to see if he was willing to work on my car in the near future. He could, but he wanted me to come and show him the car so that he could check what needed to be done. I asked my girlfriend to come with me, which is very unusual as I rarely require any support to do things. I have always been a girl who felt that I can manage to do things on my own. But the thing is that my girlfriend had said many times that I should meet this Roger, who was a friend of her husband. The reason was that she thought he was very nice and kind and thought that we would get along well. I wasn't at all impressed with the proposal and waved it off with the comment that I wasn't interested in someone who likes motorcycles... Don't ask me why I thought that...

We decided on a day when my girlfriend and I would go to

Roger's garage to show him my car – August 9, 2013. When I stepped out of the car in the workshop yard and saw Roger come walking toward us I knew at that moment that this was the man I had been waiting for and who was "meant" for me. We shook hands and greeted each other politely and I could still feel strongly that this was him with a capital H. ☺ Afterwards, Roger told me that he also knew when he saw me that this was probably something more than just a "regular customer" that came with their car for service. He also said that his grandmother always said that he would marry a red-headed woman. I'm not a natural redhead, but have for the most part colored my hair red and did so even at this time.

Roger, who was currently living in another relationship, said nothing more on the issue and I didn't think that something more would happen between us, but he did complete the car service and he said I was welcome back if I had a problem with the car again.

What none of us quite understood at the time was that we would be seeing each other quite often after this as my car took the matter into its own hands and saw to it that I needed to visit the garage and Roger often. The car made a strange sound and the lights needed bulb replacements very often. This resulted in that I spent a lot of time in the garage, and when the job was done I often stayed and kept talking with Roger. It felt as if we could talk about everything and it was never hard to find topics to discuss. At the same time it felt as if we had known each other for a long time, despite the fact that we had only recently met. We also found out that we had been at the same party about 1 year ago, but neither of us could remember that we had seen each other at the party. We usually joke and say that it would be fun to know how many hours I spent in the garage, but at the same time it gave us the opportunity to get to know each other. Although as I have said, it already felt as if we did, inside and out. Roger kept working on the cars and I made coffee for us and watched him fix the cars and served sometimes as handyman with tools etc. At some point we started to give each other a hug when we parted and it was like the most natural thing in the whole world. Both probably felt the chemistry that was there between us, but we were very careful with putting it into words at the beginning.

At this stage I was absolutely sure that this Roger was the man I wanted to live with and the question was how it would be possible when he lived in a different relationship. His current partner was also very sick at this time and I felt that I couldn't push him too much one way or the other. Instead, I was there as a good friend and listener when and if he needed it. I went for AT Balancing sessions during the autumn of 2013 with Johanna Saari, the Aura Mediator Instructor™ in Finland, who confirmed the same things that I had been wondering about, i.e., that Roger was my Spirit Mate, but that the time wasn't right for the two of us yet. It was very hard to accept and embrace this, when I most of all would have married him instantly. I found a small consolation in Anni and Carsten's book about Spirit Mates, and that helped me wait out the situation.

In October of 2013 I told Roger how I felt about him and made it clear to him that I was prepared to wait for him. I felt, however, that for my own sake I also had to try to let go a little, and try to live on until the time was ripe for the two of us. It was quite difficult to have strong feelings for someone who wasn't available at the moment. After this, for different reasons there was a small break in our relationship, but perhaps mainly because my car didn't have anything wrong with it for about 2 months, so I had no reason to visit the garage during this time.

Around Christmas we were once again at the same party and

Roger told me that he first hadn't intended to go to the party, but decided at the last minute to go after all, just in case I would be there. During the evening I felt as if we were a bit on the path toward our shared goal, but we had a way to go yet.

After this meeting my car started needing service again and even my mom's car suddenly had a lot wrong with it that needed to be fixed in Roger's garage. ☺ The ball was simply rolling again, and I again spent countless hours at the garage.

In early April of 2014, I went to the Planet course held by Anni Sennov in Helsinki, Finland. I remember when she asked how I was feeling that I answered that I would be in need of a Balancing session. She replied with a big smile that after the course weekend, I'd probably feel like I did a Balancing session and even be in balance. And she knew very well what she was talking about as a few days later, Roger sent me a message late one night, and it was the start of our shared journey and future together.

Barely two weeks later, we were living together, and after one day of living together Roger proposed to me and gave me a ring, and there was no doubt about what I answered. ☺ Most of our surroundings were very excited for our sake and said that we finally had, especially Roger, come to our senses and settled the matter. ☺ They meant that people had seen that we had marital likeness for each other.

But it was also a pretty turbulent period as a lot happened in a short period of time. Roger went through a separation, and separations aren't always painless, with all that that entails. Both Roger and I were very happy together and everything felt so right, but because so much happened all the time, we were both rather tired and sometimes exhausted. Our bodies began to react physically in different ways; I started having migraines, which I never had trouble with before, and Roger had major problems with his back. But we understood what it was about and tried to relax and cut down on the tough pace that was going on around us at the time, and gradually the symptoms subsided and things calmed down.

Roger says that when the relationship is right, you have the energy to get through stormy situations. According to him, the foundation of our relationship is honesty, trust and acceptance, as well as permission to be the person you are, and loved for who you are.

On Walpurgis Night in 2014, which is an official bonfire day in Finland, Sweden and several other European countries, we were a large gang at a local pub in our small town and an orchestra played beautiful music, and among other things, love ballads. During one song, which I unfortunately don't remember, I told Roger that I had always hoped and thought that I would get married before I turned 40 years old, which I would be the following year. But since I met Roger, it felt as if I could get married immediately, at once. Roger replied with a big smile that the previous night he dreamt about the number 21. I personally am very spontaneous and took out my phone and looked at the calendar to see when the date 21 fell on a Saturday during the coming summer. To my delight, it wasn't so far off; it was Midsummer Day, June 21, 2014. I said this to Roger and asked him if we were going to get married at Midsummer. When he immediately answered yes, there were no words to describe the happiness I felt. Nor the love and gratitude I felt to have met Roger, who according to me is the finest and the most wonderful man in the world. ☺

The following day, May 1, we were out eating at a restaurant with my girlfriend Camilla and her family. Camilla was the one who said I should meet Roger and who came with me when I went to show my car to him the first time. We told her and her family that we were going to get married in 7 weeks (!) and even asked if we could have the wedding reception in the gardens at their summer house, which they gladly said we could. Now, planning and setting up was done at a fairly rapid pace as 7 weeks isn't a long time when it comes to all of what it means to have a wedding.

When I told Roger about AuraTransformation™, he became very interested and wanted to also do an AT. We consulted Anni, via Johanna Saari, and Anni recommended Roger do an AT before we got married to avoid many different problems on soul level following us into marriage. Roger did an AT in May of 2014. There was no major change in our relationship after Roger's AT, but it perhaps strengthened the wonderful feeling and happiness we felt together even more. Everything felt so right, even the sexual part got even better as we both felt that it was both deeper and stronger, and the feeling that two became one was very noticeable. We both agree 100 percent with what the book, "Spirit Mates – The New Time Relationship" says: that the key words in relationships are intuition, love, security and trust! ♡

On June 19, 2014 we were married by a judge at the registry office in our neighboring city of Ekenäs. It was a small, fine event with those closest to us, and we celebrated afterwards by eating a wedding lunch at a restaurant. Two days later, on Midsummer's Day, we had our wedding reception outdoors as planned. The weather, however, wasn't really on our side as it went from being almost high summer warm to suddenly changing and being only 10 degrees Celsius and windy. But it didn't matter and our guests were provided with warm clothing, and the atmosphere at the party was very warm and cozy. Then after midnight there even came a lot of hail so that the ground turned white, which we saw only as a sign of good luck. ☺

One day we experienced an example of how it is to live with your Spirit Mate. I was at home and Roger was at work that day when my phone suddenly plings and up comes a reminder that says "Call Roger." I didn't understand anything because I had not added this reminder. I called Roger at once, however, and told him what had happened. Right then he was in the car at the gas station and had just finished filling the tank to go to the neighboring town and get some car parts that he needed for work. When he heard what had just happened, he told me that last night he had dreamt that he was hit in his car by a bus and just when the bus hit him in the dream he woke up. How the dream ended, he would never know... We decided that it was best that he didn't go to the neighboring town that day, because it seemed as if there clearly were clear signs that he shouldn't go. The following day he called me shortly after he arrived at work and told me that he had been backed into by a large truck at an intersection. The truck that stood still at the crossing had suddenly put it in reverse and backed straight into Roger who was sitting in the car behind, completely without warning. Luckily no one was hurt, just a little bodily damage, which was easy to fix. We are fully convinced that these incidents were connected and are so grateful that the phone helped us with the message. We dare not even think what would have happened otherwise.

At the beginning of the summer, we also got a great offer to move to a single house in our town. Before the summer was over, we had put our town house up for sale and moved into the house. As you can see, things happened all the time, and in retrospect it wasn't strange that we were tired and sometimes exhausted, when everything happened so fast and so much happened in a short time. ☺ In connection with the move, I found the envelope with all the qualities I'd written down of what I wished for in my future husband. Every single attribute that was on the paper – and there were about 25

– Roger had all of them. ☺

What is it that makes a relationship between Spirit Mates so special? We think that the feeling you have that you have come home, found the right person, is indescribable. Many times we think the same thing without even saying anything to each other. And there is a huge trust and security between us. As there aren't many things to fight about, it's rare that we fight. Of course we can have different opinions, but our differences are in some way also our similarities.

When we look back on the three years we've been together, we usually say that we've been through a lot in such a short time. At the same time, it feels as if we've known each other a long time and even been together a lot longer than three years. That being said, a lot has happened in these three years; we met and got married, and our son Edwin was born in January of 2016. And our daughter Elwira was born in April of 2017. Right now we are living and enjoying to the fullest every moment of being parents of two beautiful Crystal-Golden energy children. ♡

Roger says he always wanted to meet the right one, and to have children and pets. He had never thought before we met three years ago that he would now be the father of two, and have his own dog. He also expanded his business more than a year ago, and the business has multiplied and currently employs three workers.

We have many shared interests, especially health and well-being, which we are both passionate about.

Our advice to anyone wishing to meet their Spirit Mate is to not give up. They will come when it's time for you to meet and when you are ready for it. And in the end it's worth all the waiting, we promise! ☺

With love, Ewa-Lotta & Roger Bergström

When the family energy takes over

As you can sense from reading Ewa-Lotta and Roger's love story, they have a wonderful balance in their relationship and family, which is usually much easier to have when your children are small. When the children grow older, many challenging situations can occur in the family like you have read about in Annelie and Jörgen's love story (# 4).

It's hard for all parents who love each other to deal with children who are seriously ill, no matter the child's age, but there is often much more in it for Spirit Mates than for most other parents. When a Spirit Mates love couple has such experiences and challenges with their children, it usually has something to do with the couple's common life purpose, like it did in Anna and Ola's love story (# 1) when their eldest son was diagnosed with leukemia at the age of three.

On top of everything else that goes on in the Spirit Mates couple's common life and energies, they must deal with the family energy that tries to take over the control of their relationship energy, which can be a very difficult situation to handle for the couple. Not many parents will let other people take care of their children if the children have trouble, just because they'd rather spend time together with their love partner. That's not how things usually work, so when the children are sick or need their parents to be around all the time, the love relationship energy of the Spirit Mates couple has to be on standby, which can be extremely hard for the two Spirit Mates to deal with in their respective energy systems and bodies.

Often, it's much easier for the couple to close the door between their respective energies and have a long break from their mutual integration process, than it is to open and close the door all the time not knowing what to expect from time to time.

Just imagine a Spirit Mates love couple that needs to be together all the time to merge their energies, because they come from opposite directions in life and the start-up phase took time like it did for Annelie and Jörgen. They needed to spend time in a common bubble of calm and balance, so their auras could melt together, and they felt empty inside when they were not together. They simply felt that they lacked a part of themselves when their love partner was not around, and furthermore, they had lots of resistance coming from the outside world at the beginning of their relationship. They also had to learn to speak the same language, because they had very different ways of expressing themselves in the first years they were together, so they must have felt really bad when Annelie's youngest daughter went to the hospital, where it was required that Annelie was around her all the time.

There was only one thing they could do to save their relationship: They had to agree to always be honest with each other and wait for each other in the same way as people would do if they lived in different places on Earth and had no possibility of being in the same place.

A family crisis created the basis for bringing their relationship to a new level with greater involvement from both parties, and when they chose each other 100%, everything became perfect between them. However, when the family crisis was over, they had become so used to living with conflicts and problems in their daily lives and supporting others, that they could not figure out how to navigate in a balanced way in their love relationship.

Now is was Jörgen's turn to work on his former life, which Annelie was forced to do when she got sick earlier in the relationship, and a new crisis emerged which separated the couple and caused them to hurt each other. Fortunately, they chose to stay in the relationship and to support each other, regardless of what they had exposed each other to, as forgiveness is a very natural part of a Spirit Mates relationship.

So even if you live together with your one and only love partner, there can be such big challenges in the family, that it can be hard for the Spirit Mates energy to expand, and then it can be easier for the love couple to separate their energies for a period of time and wait for a better timing, where they can merge their energies completely.

It doesn't necessarily mean that the family energy or the children's energies have won over the Spirit Mates energy, because that is not the case. Instead, Annelie and Jörgen's Spirit Mates Integration Process shows how important it is to do as much of the personal development work as possible before you meet, because otherwise everything will happen with such great power during the Spirit Mates Integration Process when the couple lives together.

Answers to the most frequently asked questions about Spirit Mates

When we started the writing of this book we invited our readers to ask questions about Spirit Mates that we could answer in this book.

Most of the questions we received were already on our list of what we wanted to write about and/or have been answered in the 10 love stories that we share with you in our book. Other questions will be answered here even though we have not used a standard Q & A setup:

- People rarely get hints about who their Spirit Mate is before they meet because they usually don't sense and see their own energy in another person.

- Waiting for your Spirit Mate is the most difficult phase of the relationship, but as soon as you meet and your respective consciousnesses are fused together, and you have entered into a deep love relationship with each other, you will know that things could not have been in a different way with a good result.

- A Spirit Mates relationship is drama-free and if this is not the case for you, you have either met each other too soon or you are not Spirit Mates. Spirit Mates seldom react in an uncontrolled way towards each other unless it's about life and death. Then they'd rather focus inwardly and keep silent. Most Spirit Mates love couples prefer to face reality instead of living their life based on an illusion, and as soon as a challenge is solved, it's time for the love couple to move on and enjoy life again.

- Only you can know for sure if you have met or are together with your Spirit Mate. Don't always rely on what you are being told by spiritual counselors.

- Spirit Mates look alike, which you can see in all the Spirit Mates couple photos that we share in this book. There are so many similarities between the love couples, whether it's their look, personal energy or radiance. Spirit Family members also look alike, which is why the extra parents and children that come with a divorce and remarry situation often look more like each other than biological parents and children.

  You can read more about the term Spirit Family in the next chapter, as well as in Anni's book "Golden Age, Golden Earth."

- There is an energy copy of your Spirit Mate inside of you just like there is an energy copy of you inside of your Spirit Mate, so you are always connected in spirit no matter if you have met in physical life or not.

- If you have met your Spirit Mate in real life and you must separate for some reason, the energies that have already been merged together will still be merged at spirit level until you meet again. In this way the Spirit Mates Integration Process will continue at a spiritual level, and you will be prepared in each your own way to connect as a love couple later on.

  You might think that the integration process would be easier and smoother if you were living together on a daily basis, but you should always trust your own spirit more than your brain. Your spirit has a divine wide-screen perspective, whereas your brain has a mental, logical and creative perspective that will help you figure out how and what to do to meet and unite with your Spirit Mate, but that is not how things work spiritually.

You cannot figure out what to do to meet your Spirit Mate. You can only have a look at yourself and see what is missing inside, and when there is a full match in spirit between the two of you, everything will settle. If there is not a full match, you can be standing at the right place in front of the "love door" to your Spirit Mate, but the key will not match yet.

Also notice that timing is a very important factor, so you can actually be ready and still have to wait a few more days or weeks before you finally meet.

- When Spirit Mates are searching for each other here on Earth, they can easily happen to meet partners who match their energy 70%, 80% and 90%. This happens in order to gradually prepare their energy systems to meet their own energy in another body that matches their spirit energy 100%.

There might not be as many problems in these relationships as there would if the love partners were true Consciousness Mates, where problems usually occur within a very short time.

- If one Spirit Mate has a big longing to meet the other half of themselves, this will also be the case for the other Spirit Mate. This is not just a one-sided feeling. However, there can be circumstances in the lives of both Spirit Mates or just one of them, that will keep them separated for a longer time than they hope for. But you can be sure that none of the Spirit Mates will risk "falling asleep," so they don't meet each other, unless they are very old and not supposed to connect at soul level in this life. If, however, they have both raised their energies to spirit level, they will for sure meet each other at spirit level in one way or another.

- Many people believe that we are all Spirit Mates and we absolutely agree. We are just not all Spirit Mates with each other.

  Initially, we all originate from the same divine source, but we do not originate from the same cell division. That's the reason why there is such a big difference between people on this Earth, and therefore many people cannot relate to each other and would for sure never be love partners with each other.

- It is possible for a person at spirit level to be attracted to more love/sex partners at the same time, but energy-wise the person only has one Spirit Mate. The other love/sex partners may instead be soul friends or belong to the person's Spirit Family.

- There is no difference in the energies of heterosexual, homosexual and transsexual relationships. However in the physical world, it's all about the gender and looks and how people live their lives.

  Love is love, no matter if it's between women and men, or two women or two men, and homosexual and transsexual people can be as much Spirit Mates as heterosexual people.

We are influenced by the energies of our planet

On Planet Earth we are all surrounded by so many diverse energies that we cannot embrace them all if we try to integrate them as one energy. Therefore, the overall energies of our planet have been divided into different types of energies such as the Masculine and Feminine energies, the 4 Elements (Fire, Water, Earth and Air), the 13 Dimensions, the Planetary energies belonging to the outskirts of Planet Earth, as well as different types of human and spiritual relationships, etc., that are much easier terms for the human brain to understand and relate to.

One thing, however, that is not complicated at all for the human brain, and for the heart to understand and accept, is that every person on this planet must find their "Perfect Heart Match" at spirit level to feel whole. Fortunately, this is now possible due to the presence of the high-frequency Golden energy and life force that was released and activated with the end of the Mayan Calendar on the 21st December 2012. Huge amounts of Golden life force and materialization power have been released in our beautiful planet and this energy will help all people to embrace and love each other much more than has ever been possible before.

Love has always been here, but the spiritual frequency of the love energy that is now accessibe for all humans is so high-frequency, and the love potential and capacity found in Planet Earth is now so big, that it will sweep you off your feet. And what's even more amazing is that it will be even bigger when more Spirit Mates couples meet as love couples in physical life. Meeting your Spirit Mate is a very unique and amazing way to raise the overall love energy on our planet.

If you want to know more about why and how you should raise your personal energy, so it matches the new era on Planet Earth called "The Golden Age," we recommend that you read Anni's book "Golden Age, Golden Earth." It's simply too complicated for us to try to mix the information about the two extremely fascinating topics "Spirit Mates" and "The Golden Age" in one and the same book with the purpose of giving you an overview of how they are connected energy-wise. As we see it, there is no reason for making things more complicated than they need to be, and Anni has already written several books on the mentioned topics that describe them so well and seen from different perspectives.

In her book "Golden Age, Golden Earth," she has written about Planetary energies and the Masculine and Feminine energies as well as the 4 Elements. She has also written about the different relationship types that are found on our planet like Soul Mates, Consciousness Mates and Spirit Mates, which are all mentioned in this book. However, the terms *Soul Friends, Spirit Family* and *Source Duals*, which are very important relationship types in the lives of many people, have not yet been described in this book. Therefore, we have written a short explanation below, so you can better understand the difference between these terms and the term "Spirit Mates."

Soul Friends

Just like Soul Mates, Soul Friends are individuals who have been together through many lives, and this has been agreed upon from one life to another. They often feel that they belong together in some way, which causes them to value their friendship very deeply.

Spirit Family

Your Spirit Family has the exact same function on spirit level as your Soul Friends have on soul level. However, the members of your Spirit Family are often very conscious that you have a deep connection on spirit level and that you have been together through many lives and eras both in the physical world and in spirit.

Some people have identical biological family and Spirit Family members, but often your Spirit Family will only consist of selected biological family members and not your whole family. Your Spirit Family can also come from outside of your biological family, and you will always follow and support each other in spirit where you are connected. However, your Spirit Family does not come from the same cell division as your Spirit Mate does.

Source Duals

A Source Dual is a dharma and life-task focused relationship that can take place between people of all ages as long as they have the same overall source in spirit on a higher level of consciousness. Source Duals belong in different places in the consciousness layers and the spiritual development chain, a bit like cousins belonging to the same family.

Source Duals are **not** Spirit Mates, and they work across the system instead of coming from the same spiritual platform as Spirit Mates do. Source Duals have life tasks equivalent to the scale of the life tasks of Spirit Mates, but their energies are not complementary like those of Spirit Mates. However, they are more alike in their human and mental energy structures, but their joint power does not grow monumentally as the joint power of Spirit Mates does.

The Masculine and Feminine energies

The Masculine and Feminine energies are the two most simplified and basic impulses that exist on Planet Earth and in the cosmos. They are the two most essential players in all materialization on Earth, where the Masculine energy represents the Creative Force, and the Feminine energy represents Creation itself – also called the Creation Force.

However, both the Creative Force and Creation contain Masculine and Feminine energy, because there is nothing on this planet that is exclusively Masculine or Feminine, and it's important for all people to understand the essence and dynamic of these two energies to better be able to balance their energies in all contexts.

The 4 Elements

The 4 Elements consist of the elements of Fire, Water, Earth and Air, which represent four different types of balance and strength that exist everywhere on and in our planet, just like the Masculine and Feminine energies.

The 4 Elements are very important for how you experience being with other people, and if you do not master your own personal element combination and you are not conscious of your own way of expressing yourself, you will most certainly not succeed when being with others, nor in your relationship(s).

Spirit Mates usually have two different element combinations that match and complement each other, so they can unite their energies in a balanced way while at the same time, be able to support and learn from each other through the part of their respective element combinations that differ from each other.

There are no element combinations that are more right than others when it comes to a Spirit Mates relationship, as it all depends on the couple's common life purpose and how they are supposed to live their mutual life. All people have the 4 Elements in different combinations, strengths and balance, and so do Spirit Mates, and it doesn't make sense for a Spirit Mates love couple to have lots of Water element if they are supposed to use the Fire element when fulfilling their common dharma. However, people rarely get a chance of meeting their Spirit Mate if they have not yet integrated the 4 Elements in a balanced way in their body and mind.

The 4 Elements, and the Planetary energies that are mentioned later, were created after the great cosmic cell division, while the Masculine and Feminine energies existed before the great cosmic cell division, where they had a very important role.

You can read much more about the 4 Elements on the website: **www.fourelementprofile.com**, and in Anni's two books "Golden Age, Golden Earth" and "The Crystal Human and the Crystallization Process I."

The 13 Dimensions

Within spiritual circles it is said that Planet Earth is about to move from the 3rd to the 5th dimension, also called 3D and 5D, which will of course influence people's choice of partnership in the future. The feeling of love in the 5th dimension is much more spiritual and universal than in the 3rd dimension, where love is perceived in a very personal and emotional way. The more conscious you are about who you are and what you want in life, the easier it is for you to be part of a high-frequency spiritual relationship.

However, we will not touch on this big subject here. Instead, we recommend that you read about the Spiritual Dimensions that exist on Planet Earth in Anni's book "The Crystal Human and the Crystallization Process Part I."

All we know is that it is a divine intention that we should all be able to live together in a Spirit Mates relationship as love partners on a physical level in a higher spiritual dimension. Therefore, Spirit Mates will for sure meet in physical life even though they can also meet in a non-physical dimension full of unconditional love. However, once you are in balance and have an open heart – which usually happens in the 5th dimension – then you will be closer to meeting and recognizing each other's energies on a physical level, where you will have a common life-purpose to fulfill.

The Planetary energies

The planetary energies of our solar system have, for the most part, been here all along, in various combinations. The planetary energies exist in everyone all over Planet Earth and many people even have energy within them that originates from planets, solar systems and galaxies outside of our own solar system. This amazing topic Anni has examined and written about in her book "Golden Age, Golden Earth" where you can read about the planetary energies in our solar system as well as influential planets outside our solar system.

Spirit Mates usually develop in the opposite direction of each other in all contexts, so they can better complement each other and one day combine their energies into one large and much more intelligent energy pool than they had when they were separated from each other in spirit. Therefore, it is very unlikely for them to have the exact same planetary energies.

Michael and Crystal Ra

Love Story # 7

When and how did you meet?

We met at the end of 2014 in La Cruz de Huanacaxtle, a little fishing village just outside of Puerto Vallarta. Originally from Estonia, Crystal Ra had spent years traveling the world before settling in Mexico. She was in La Cruz to visit with friends and heal after a relationship ended. Michael, an American who had also done his fair share of traveling, was going through major life changes as well. He was in La Cruz to see friends and work on his boat. The first time they were in each other's company they did not officially meet; once they did, though, it was as if they'd known each other for years.

Background to Crystal Ra's story

World travel has always been a passion of mine. I love going to new places, meeting new people and immersing myself in new cultures. Eventually I ended up in Mexico, which was where I met Michael at the end of 2014. In those days, the only traveling I did was from Mazatlán to La Cruz, where I went to heal and reset my life after a bad breakup. At that time, I was not looking for "Mr. Perfect"; my last relationship had been rather toxic, and I had decided I was done searching for romance and would instead "marry" my job. I truly enjoyed it and if work was to be the focal point of my life, that was fine.

Fate had different plans for me, however. It wasn't until after Michael and I met that I remembered my visit to Estonia the year before. It was Christmastime, and everywhere one looked there were beautiful evergreens, red and green lights... and Santa Clauses. When a Santa asked what I wanted for Christmas, I answered his question with a question: "Are you taking orders for men?" He said he was, so I sat down in a café to write down my "ordering list" – consisting of all the qualities I was looking for in a partner. Two hours later, I tried to find the Santa but he was already gone.

It was about one year later when Michael showed up – literally on my doorstep! Sure, Santa had been late with my present, but considering how much I moved around, he probably had trouble finding my address!

Background to Michael's story

For years, Mexico has been a place of new and wonderful beginnings for me. It began in 2007, when I sold everything I owned in Southern California, jumped on my sailboat and headed south. Before long, the Pacific Coast of Mexico had become my second home. When Crystal Ra and I met in 2014, I was separating from my wife of twenty-two years and had returned to Mexico to process, reflect and look for healing.

The meeting

Michael: The first time I spotted Crystal Ra, she was sitting at a table with some friends. I was close by, and though I could feel a strong sense of her presence and found it mysterious and inviting, I did not approach her. The next day, after being introduced by a mutual acquaintance, we started talking in the café area, then Crystal Ra invited me upstairs to see the view of the village.

Crystal Ra: As we chatted, I wondered why Michael kept saying "we," as he did not have a wedding ring on. It became clear when Michael shared a bit of his recent life story and the emotional heartache of breaking up with his wife of twenty-two years.

He expressed the need for some intense healing, and we

scheduled appointments for many different healing modality sessions over the next two weeks. One of the sessions was an AuraTransformation™. I felt this in-depth healing would help Michael to get clarity about his new life faster than anything else.

Have you had an AuraTransformation™ already or did you have it after you met, and if so, how did this change your relationship?

Crystal Ra: I had my AuraTransformation™ in February 2007 in Northern Norway. In the years that followed, I had met many consciousness partners, fell in love, broke up and moved on. It was always the same story, and it exhausted me. I had started to think something was wrong with me because I was not able to find my Spirit Mate. But what I realized was that all these consciousness partners had cleared my patterns so I would be ready for Michael to come into my life. By the time we met I was starting the last phase of my body crystallization, where the energy frequency in my body was upgraded to spirit level.

At this time, I was very broken emotionally. My employer had abused me verbally, emotionally and even physically. There had been warning signs when I took the position, but I chose it because I was promised a roof over my head, food in my belly, and the opportunity to do what I loved. I soon found myself with no money of my own, no car, no internet, and no phone. I was living in total fear.

Now, looking back, I understand that I had to experience such a situation, because I had to get to the very rock bottom to find enough will and energy to rise from the ashes. It was part of my transformation.

That said, I still had some work to do. Michael said from the very beginning that he does not do well with drama, so I had to clear my old patterns in order to be with him. Part of this process was going to Al-Anon, a support program for people whose lives have been affected by someone else's alcohol or substance abuse. Both of my parents were alcoholics, and as a result I'd had relationships with other addicts. These meetings were very helpful, even more so because Michael often accompanied me.

Most of my previous male partners were always so insecure and putting me down. Here I had a true king, who is a born leader, entrepreneur and a caring person who supported me in my efforts to work on myself. That was completely new to me.

Michael: I'm not sure whether the AuraTransformation™ changed our relationship that moment, but I do know that it helped to create a foundation for our future. The first twelve months of our relationship had many ups and downs, which in and of itself was not unusual, but Crystal Ra explained that this process was accelerated because I had been transformed. All I can say is it helped me to make that transition complete and make peace with it and move forward toward the future.

Was it love at first sight or when did you find out?

Crystal Ra: I was instantly drawn to Michael; his energy was so yummy I wanted to hug and kiss him. I felt so "at home" with him. But I also remembered my decision not to jump into another relationship too quickly. So I played it cool, knowing that if we wanted to make it work we needed to heal more of our past wounds. Over time, and despite challenges and physical distance, I gradually fell in love with him. I wanted to be with him all the time, and best of all, the feeling was mutual.

Michael: It was not love at first sight, but Crystal Ra's euphoric energy immediately made me feel comfortable. It made me want to investigate who she was. It made me want to hug and hold her.

We both felt the chemistry and we explored it. Yet we also understood that it would take more than that to make a relationship sustainable. We needed common goals, compatibility, friendship and love. That is what the first year gave us – many opportunities to explore the various facets of each other and find out how well we fit together.

How did you know this was different and/or when did you find out?

Crystal Ra: I felt it from the very beginning. Michael is a true gentleman, with a regal, polite and caring presence unlike any man I'd ever known. I also noticed that what he said and did was always aligned. He was not living a lie – he did not try to be someone he was not. He was very supportive in everything I did or was challenged with.

Three weeks after we met Michael brought up the possibility of a relationship; he even spoke about moving in together. Though my heart was jumping with joy, I knew it was too early to do that and so I kept my individual platform in place. Yet, no matter how much I resisted, I couldn't deny the powerful energetic pull towards him. I estimated it would take at least a year for both of us to heal and figure out whether we were on the same path, and I was right.

Michael: I knew it was different from the beginning just because I felt her energy, but feeling it and learning about it was new to me and opened doors to things I had never experienced before. Before meeting her, my life was completely different – more rational. Now she was introducing me to the spiritual lifestyle, a life of energy reading and magic that I found very exciting. I was opened, interested and thirsty for learning more about the world Crystal Ra was part of and what it had to offer.

I also noticed that Crystal Ra appreciated me like no one else. She recognized and honored not only who I was internally, but the way I expressed it. I could see in the depth of her eyes that love and desire, the glow which made me feel compelled to be more and do more.

How did you know you were Spirit Mates?

Crystal Ra: To answer this question I have to go back to my childhood in Soviet Estonia. Life was not easy there; many of the men had been lost to wars, deportation and death, and as a result the women had to take on traditionally masculine roles. They had to be very strong in order to survive. That pattern, and growing up with a very powerful, tough grandmother, made me into a survivor power woman who unfortunately attracted very weak men. Most times I ended up taking care of them, paying for them, offering them a roof over their heads and so on. Sometimes I even became their driver.

When Michael came into my life I immediately sensed a very different energy, but not wanting to be disappointed once again, I decided to test him. For the first year after we met, I got many opportunities to do so.

To my surprise, Michael did not leave me; in fact, these challenges only brought us closer together. Then I knew that he must be something more special than a consciousness partner.

Michael: When Crystal Ra asked me this question for the first time, I quipped, "Because you told me so."

She laughed and said, "This is such a Michael joke."

All kidding aside, I believe we are Spirit Mates because of all the thoughts, feelings, ideas and desires we share. Our individual desires are amplified tenfold because they come together as a common goal, something we are working for as a team. We want to share our life together, we want to make this world a better place for others as well as ourselves. Perhaps most importantly, there is a depth of feeling – we feel we have known each other before – as well as the rare sense of comfort, peace and calm we feel as we experience life together, that makes me believe we are Spirit Mates.

What has happened in your life since you met?

Crystal Ra: During our first year we were testing each other and figuring out who we are as individuals as well as a unit. I personally think we may have been brought together by the spirit a bit early (in fact, we broke up three times during that first year), but in retrospect I think this adjustment period was necessary for us to work out all the "bugs" on every level.

This was a particularly challenging time for me. Michael had gone back to his ex-wife to see if their marriage could be saved. After all, he had invested twenty-two years in the relationship and was not about to give up on it so easily. I was devastated, and for several months we did not communicate at all. I even blocked him on Facebook. Despite my sadness, I decided to use this time as an opportunity to get very clear on who I am and what I want and what works for me in a relationship. I even created what I called my "Self Declaration" list.

The first point on my list: I will not date married men anymore, unless their partner is informed that I am in the picture and is okay with it, or if he brings me his divorce papers. Shortly after I wrote this, Michael reached out to tell me he had gotten divorced. I was heading back to Mexico after a visit to Estonia, and he asked if we could meet back at the same cultural center where we had met.

Determined to take care of myself, I vowed that I would not be intimate with him again until he showed me the divorce papers. After the papers came we started something I called a "love internship." For the next two and a half months, we kept separate rooms at the cultural center, but spent a lot of time together, getting to know each other better.

After the trial period had passed, we created a five-page relationship agreement, which we both signed. He then headed off to work in Alaska for five months, and I took off to Estonia. During that time I visited him in Alaska, and later, in California while he promoted his newly released book, "Dreams, Goals and Adventure."

After this we traveled to Hawaii for a couple of months, where I was doing one of my adventure retreats. At this point I had been location-free since 2011, and Michael had been so since 2007. We were now both looking for a place to call home, and as Hawaii was on my list, I wanted Michael to see it and figure out if he would love it too.

After Hawaii we visited Michael's parents in Palm Springs, California, then returned to Mexico, where I had set up my new company and was offering my water therapy modality, Wantra. Michael was working a bit with his real estate projects.

Michael: That first year is a whole book in itself. It was on and off a lot. Then, when we decided to give it a go, we built our individual platforms first and then slowly put one foot on our common platform together at the same time so there would be balance and strength. We did not want to upset any of the platforms or lose ourselves individually, but to strengthen our individual and unified presences.

Our individual platforms are who we are – our strengths, our weaknesses, the good and bad. Our common platform is the combination of our efforts, experiences and knowledge, knowing that there will be trials and tribulations that will challenge and strengthen our individual platforms so we can deal with all of life's events. Individually and together, we are stronger.

Through the intense transitional process, I had to let go of the past. This meant not only saying goodbye to that long marriage, but also the material things like the boat and real estate holdings we'd shared so I could start over with a clean slate.

Even more difficult was dealing with the feeling that I had let my ex-wife down. I reflected on the relationship, wondering what I might have done to cause this separation from a woman I'd once believed was my life partner.

Eventually I realized there was no "fault" involved. Despite our best efforts, a breakdown in communication had occurred. Since then I have learned that there is more than one love language and I have taken that knowledge and applied it in my new relationship with Crystal Ra. The result is a more nourishing and complete bond than I have ever had before.

Tell about some real-life incidents and experiences you have had together so people can get a feeling for how it is to live together as Spirit Mates

Crystal Ra: We communicate very well with each other. There has never been a time when I felt that Michael did not care or was avoiding me, not even when we were physically separated. During those times we chatted online each day and Skyped as often as we could, letting each other know what was going on with our lives. Even when I was taking classes back in Estonia – leaving very early in the morning and getting home very late – I let Michael know by text that I had made it safely.

In many of my previous relationships I always felt there were certain topics I could not even bring up. Michael and I can talk about anything, and when one of us is facing a challenge, the other is always there offering support.

The main difference, though, is that there is no conflict, no drama and no unconscious assuming or patterns going on. If something comes up we've agreed to talk about it right away so we do not suppress it. That is a huge difference for me from past experiences. It makes life so much happier and healthier.

I also feel Michael is behind me and supporting me in whatever I do. Michael is very confident in himself and mature, so he always uplifts me in every possible way instead of putting me down. That makes me feel so good and proud of him too.

Michael: Crystal Ra and I are a team on every level. Oftentimes, we are on the same mission and working towards the same goals without even realizing it! Yet we still make it a habit of sitting down to discuss it. This way we're sure to stay on point and work through any differences so we can come up with the best possible outcome for both of us. We always bring equality to the table, always honor each other and each other's ideas.

We have also built a rock solid, mutual trust. Crystal Ra is very supportive of any ideas or actions I might take, knowing I will always have our best interest in mind, and I feel the same about her. We are also both very conscious of communicating our needs or concerns because we know this is key to a happy and healthy relationship. Finally, our cultural differences create an opportunity to learn from and grow through each other.

What is so special about your relationship that you haven't experienced in any previous relationship?

Crystal Ra: For me it has been a totally different quality on every level, including consciousness, communication and energetically. Those first few months with Michael I was almost addicted to him. I needed to be very close to him and touch him and I loved to make love to him. We hardly got out of bed! My body, my heart and my whole being was expanding each time we made love. I felt like I was melting.

As I mentioned earlier, the support Michael has given me is unlike anything I have experienced before. Michael is a true gentleman – opening the doors or carrying heavy stuff for me is second nature to him – which has made me feel like a true queen for the first time in my life. He is also the first man who didn't leave when a true challenge appeared. He is a warrior in his heart.

Michael and I also complement each other. He is a much more logical thinker than me, and in offering his point of view he has helped me to be more deliberate in my personal and professional choices. At the same time, his life mission is aligned with mine, which means we can co-create in ways I was never able to do in previous relationships.

Another huge difference is that we always resolve issues as quickly as possible. We do not drag it on or suppress it. This keeps the emotional levels clean and helps us maintain balance and eliminate suffering. Communication is the key and it has taken some time to figure out how to do it in a very soft and mellow way, as we both have our past wounds and weaknesses as well. Time has helped us to do that with patience and presence. We live in gratitude for what we have, rather than focusing on what we do not. In doing so, we are constantly attracting more good into our lives.

Michael: Before meeting Crystal Ra, my desire to help people was just a seed. Now that seed has begun to flourish, developing into a plan in which we can empower others to change their lives.

Crystal Ra has opened up my mind and made me see, feel and use my spiritual abilities to create new possibilities on many more levels. This has also enhanced all aspects of our relationship from work, play and pleasure.

We are also compatible on an elemental level. In the past Crystal Ra attracted men with stronger Air and Water elements, which usually meant their strengths were not compatible with hers. I have a strong Earth element, which gives Crystal Ra a platform to grow and embody her authentic womanhood.

How have people around you reacted to your relationship?

Crystal Ra: I was reluctant in the beginning to announce that we were a couple, as Michael was just divorced and I did not want it to look like I was the cause or that it happened too soon.

That said, I don't recall that anyone was against our relationship, just surprised. Many were shocked when Michael's previous marriage, which had appeared "perfect," ended so suddenly. There was also a bit of confusion during his book promotion, as the book talked about his wife and I was there with him to present it.

As for my friends, they were all very happy that I had found a new man, who was so very smart and innovative as well as kind and loving towards me.

Michael: All my friends and family let me know that if something makes me happy, then they are extremely happy for me. My mom said she loved Crystal Ra, even before she met her, for that same reason. The more they get to know her, the more they love her.

Do you work together on any common projects or do you have separated work lives?

We have both. We are still working on making both of our individual platforms strong and solid. Michael is working on his book promotion and restarting his real estate business here in Hawaii, while Crystal Ra has continued her online classes and energy healing work.

Together we are collaborating on projects that are dear to our hearts and allow us to utilize our unique abilities and experiences. Michael is very strong with planning, structure and systems as well as negotiations and contracts, while Crystal Ra uses her intuitive skills to evaluate circumstances and divine timing.

Our future goal is to have a holistic healing retreat center on the Big Island of Hawai'i, where we can help people create better lives. We plan to offer various energy modalities, workshops, classes, specialized programs and equipment to help to balance and heal the mind, body and spirit in keeping with the development of the New Time Energies. We will also offer customized retreats at designated locations around the world.

Do you have common interests?

Yes, we have many. We both love to sail, be in the water or on the water. Michael has sailed for many years and Crystal Ra's father was a sailor, so she grew up on boats and spent most of her summers in boatyards and harbors. We are both going to do more stand-up paddle boarding together.

We also love surfing and free diving, and we never miss an opportunity to swim with the wild dolphins. We love to travel, and we love to inspire and motivate others. We love community and contribute to the communities where we are. We love to watch movies together. We love to read books together. We love to explore together and go to new places, countries, and nature landscapes.

Do you have any suggestions or advice to others that would like to find their Spirit Mate?

First and foremost, work on your personal platform – figure out who you are, why you are here, what you like, what you do not like, what works and what does not work for you on your terms. Fall in love with yourself, so much so that you're not only "okay" with being alone, but love it. Then your personal individual platform is ready and balanced.

Find out your life mission, your dharma. Once you find even one little bit of that, your magnetism will get so much stronger, which in turn will activate the pull towards your Spirit Mate.

We were both in the space of not looking for someone and we think that is another important detail. If you are in panic and looking for someone you may even push them away energetically.

Michael: Do not try to force something that is not natural, because the true Spirit Mate will appear when the time is right. Also, do not let the challenges automatically discourage you from pursuing somebody if you feel they are your Spirit Mate. As Crystal Ra and I have learned, these challenges may be in place to make sure that you are true Spirit Mates. This process, while trying at times, has made us stronger while building a foundation for a happy future together.

When the timing is right you can't escape it

**Anything that is rightfully connected in spirit
can never be separated by any human on Earth.**

No matter how much magic you use, it is impossible to separate those particles and elements that belong together in spirit. Similarly, it is impossible to continue to keep particles and elements from joining if they have exactly the same spiritual source.

If the separation between various particles and people with the same spiritual source was constantly maintained, it would never be possible to lead the universes back to their origin out in the cosmos. Then we might as well abandon all spiritual development and enlightenment here on Earth. Therefore, you cannot stop or slow down the development process in any Spirit Mates' relationship, even if the couple has major challenges during the transition from soul to spirit level.

What needs to be learned and understood as an individual, must be in place for the love couple to meet as Spirit Mates at spirit level, and unfortunately there are no easy ways to get there. You cannot convince your brain to believe in something that you don't understand the essence of deep in your heart. Therefore, you cannot change your life perspective overnight just because you want to meet and connect with your Spirit Mate. A lot of things that you might not even think about have to be in place and in balance for you to meet your one and only love partner. Those things are all gathered in one and the same place – your body – and they represent different aspects of your personality, energy and consciousness.

YOU must be in balance to be able to meet your Spirit Mate in a balanced way and at an equal level. When the timing is right you simply can't avoid being connected with the other part of yourself that is placed in the body of your Spirit Mate. However, the most interesting part of it all when you finally meet, is that you know deep inside that it couldn't have happened before, because neither of you were ready for this very important love-based meeting. Meeting too soon would simply have caused too much trouble for both of you in ways that you can't imagine.

The Spirit Mates love couple, Sue and François, in the next love story, loved each other unconditionally, and they still do. Unfortunately, Sue is no longer with us in the physical world. She died of a tumor in the brain in June 2018 when we were finishing the writing of this book, and we are very grateful that François has agreed to share their love story with you, our readers, even though he misses his wife deeply and feels extremely vulnerable when thinking of her.

François is a well-known French artist, and before Sue died he painted the picture of her and him that you can see on the following page.

Sue and François

Love Story # 8

Sue: François is not a native English speaker and asked me to write our story, which he has both contributed to and approved.

When I, Sue, was quite small, I apparently said to my Grandfather "I'm going to marry a Frenchman." Whether I even knew what France was then, I'm not sure. However, I always knew that this person existed and I had a slight emptiness and longing for him, even when I was married to two other Frenchmen, disastrously, it has to be said.

I longed to really, really share myself with someone. In the deepest part of myself I knew that it was possible, but having grown up with so much trauma around relationships and with no idea as to how to have a successful one, I allowed myself to drift into cynicism.

Because of my upbringing, every relationship I had had felt like going into battle. I chose men who wanted to colonize me, make me change, make me stop asking questions, make me less intelligent, make me different, and humiliate me, often in public. François had also had two long-term relationships that had ended. He had found the end of his marriage very hard and acrimonious, as his children went to live very far away. He was so hurt, in fact, that he swore he would never marry again. He then had a long-term relationship that ended because he did not want any more children. Once, when we were in our "friends" phase he told me that he would never have another live-in relationship. He was always very protective of his children and really dedicated to giving them a wonderful upbringing. Being a good father is very important to him.

I began speaking French at around eight years old and my family spent many holidays there. If your Spirit Mate is someone that you have already met but not really noticed then maybe François and I did indeed cross paths when we were children, somewhere in France.

However, we definitely did cross paths one Sunday afternoon, at a mutual friend's house, in Lyon, France, where we were both living at the time. I felt his intensity the minute he walked in the door and he looked quite similar to my brother, who had committed suicide twenty years ago. François claims that he noticed me because I "vibrated differently" from anyone he had ever met, and because I had an asymmetrical haircut. He is an artist and therefore spends hours and hours watching matter vibrate, so there was a spark of "recognition." I, however, was in the middle of a series of horrible events and a very unpleasant break-up and he had just broken up with someone. Therefore I remained intrigued, at a distance, feeling something quite strong but not knowing what to do with it. I had been single for 5 years and was in no hurry, despite the extreme stress and loneliness of my situation, and I later learned that he had started a new relationship quite soon after this.

Our mutual friend was also an avid collector of François's work, so from time to time I would see François at exhibitions or dinners where he would look at me with such intensity that I would feel a little shy and tongue-tied. I really, really, really wanted him to like me and think that I was a good person. I also greatly admired him as an artist, knowing that he felt things extremely profoundly. He had decided very young that a conventional life was not for him; he could only be an artist and a full-time one at that. He worked every day and was always pushing the limits regarding technique. I loved that his portraits always seemed to speak volumes about the inner worlds of their subjects.

François says that he was always happy to see me but that I always appeared very distant and unfathomable.

We got to know each other a little better through our children, who all got on famously, and we gradually became friends. I hinted that maybe I would like more (a casual physical relationship) without commitment, families or anything official, but he did not get the hint. Or at least he didn't appear to.

He claims now that he felt that I was "out of his league" and that I was ultra-protective of myself. He felt that he wanted a "real" relationship and that I did not. We were quite often alone together in potentially romantic settings but never really seemed to be able to actually make overtures towards each other. We were like awkward teenagers.

One morning, having been friends with François for well over a year, I woke up just knowing that something had to happen between us. I thought about him a lot and even dreamt about him. He did not yet feel like the love of my life but I just felt that I had to act.

François says that he knew THAT he was attracted to me but that he just did not know how to approach me.

I invited him to a dinner party at the house of a couple of art collectors. He was now single again. I could feel the attraction between us growing and found it very troubling. At one point, during pre-dinner drinks, he briefly touched my leg.

It felt as if I were being sucked into an all-powerful, all-consuming vortex. It was so intense that I thought that everyone else had noticed it too. It felt dangerous yet compelling. Everyone else carried on as normal, including François. It was most disconcerting. How could they not have noticed? It was as if the world were spinning faster and faster on its axis.

To cover my confusion, I decided to go into the host's kitchen to cut some bread with a super high-tech bread knife. I promptly severed the tendon of my forefinger, which was hanging off and bleeding profusely. François took me to the hospital. As we were standing in the triage queue, I felt all the overwhelming sadness, loneliness and hopelessness that had seemed to characterize my life coming to the surface. Deep grief and self-hatred, guilt and a strong sense of not belonging. As those feelings welled up, I began to cry, at which point, François put his arm around me.

Feeling protected by a man was not something I had experienced since the death of my brother and I had resigned myself to never feeling protected by another person ever again.

François says that he realized at that point that in fact I was really vulnerable and that it created a space where he could actually get closer to me and that finally I needed something that he was able to provide. He felt very protective towards me, he says now.

It took another month for him to kiss me very quickly in his kitchen and yet another month for us to get together. When we did, I knew that I had found the man I had been aching for since childhood. François jokingly described himself as my knight in shining armor. However, that did not mean that he saw me as being weak or inferior but rather that he really cared about my happiness and well-being. What a revelation! My head really did belong on François's shoulder and all the things that I had pretended to despise about relationships began to start happening to me and to us. We could not keep our hands off each other and were consumed by the desire to be alone together...

The next two years were intense and amazing but I was still working through lots of issues and sometimes I would deliberately try to sabotage things. François had had a relatively easy upbringing and therefore found it difficult to understand some of my "knee-jerk" defensive reactions and fears of being manipulated, insulted or abused. He was always patient and kind, even when I was not. He says now that it was difficult for him to understand the extreme stress of my situation, just because it was so extreme. François believes that loyalty is a key element in our relationship. He always had my back, in every possible way and with the utmost loyalty, and this he extended to my children whom he also chose to protect and support in many different ways. I also helped out with his children. François says that I have always unconditionally supported him too.

There was some resistance to our being together. At first, François's daughter found it very hard to see her father with me. Then, the person who had introduced us that Sunday afternoon, completely dropped both François (to whom he had been very close) and me. We were absolutely totally and madly in love and everyone could see the passion and the intensity of it. Most people who knew us could see the change and rejoiced with us. Some did not, especially those who were putting up with marital situations where they were unhappy and frustrated.

Two years after our first amazing night together, I was diagnosed with a very grave illness. At that time I had a near-death experience, which, along with the illness, changed everything once again. François and I were forced to look at life differently.

It was an extremely hard time for both of us. François saw me in some terrible states. There were times when it looked as if I would not survive, yet François never flinched. He says now that he put all of his energy into pulling, pushing, pleading and cajoling me into getting better. His support gave me the strength and the resolve to choose life. My children also felt his support and kindness. I know that he felt every ounce of my pain.

Life after this shock was a quantum leap in many ways. I had been a teacher, but with the huge consciousness expansion that had happened for me, people were asking me to use clairvoyant and energy skills on them. I left my "secure" job to work with energy. François says that he always absolutely trusted me that things would work out.

François and I had never really spoken about so many things in so many different ways. I shyly began to tell François that I could see energy with the naked eye, that I could hear energy and that I knew things about people that even they did not know. When I had tried this in the past, I had been ridiculed and "rationalized" out of my own truth. Often, when I looked at François, my beloved brother would appear "through" him as if to give his approval.

When I trained as an Aura Mediator™, François asked me to transform his aura. This led to our separating for three months, as we needed to renegotiate many things. He felt that he needed to affirm himself and that is what he did. Neither of us was happy apart from the other. However, we got back together from a whole new consciousness platform once the dust had settled. We decided to get married some time after that.

After the Aura Mediator Course I had begun to understand what a Spirit Mate was. When I thought about it, I described it the following way to François. When he creates a sculpture, he always places it on an appropriate plinth. He and I together are like the right sculpture placed on the right plinth. There is perfect balance and harmony. Each part appears to be separate, yet the effect of the whole is a great deal more powerful and beautiful. The plinth complements the sculpture and vice versa. The whole cliché about being "made for each other" definitely applies!

François and I both lead with Fire and Air elements. For us, this means that we are both absolutely passionate about our respective choices of career. It also means that we are always on a quest to learn more, to go further, to understand and to create.

We both understand the other's need to work and to think deeply about work. I travel a great deal; François needs to be alone to work. Yet when I am away, I feel the strength of our Spirit and know that every cell of François's body is supporting both what I do and its greater impact. On a practical level, he puts together brochures for me and takes care of all those practical elements. I have spent a lot of time posing for him, introducing him to people who are interested in his work and talking about him!

Despite the Fire, we are very patient and kind towards each other. Hurting François would be like hurting myself. François says that he would never even think of being unkind towards me. I am always thinking of ways to make him happy. There is no jealousy, just the desire to see the other person succeed and be happy. We build each other up in times of doubt or difficulty. This is something different for us both, as our previous partners wanted us to be different from how we were.

I was brought up with the fear that if I expressed my truth I would be hated, despised, punished and humiliated. François, however, was brought up by a truly loving family and therefore he never questioned whether he was loveable. He always felt free to express himself however he chose and his parents, despite initial doubts, never thought to question his choice of being an artist. He chooses to work most days (including weekends), and to see his creative absorption and willingness to expose his deepest self through works of art is a veritable source of inspiration for me. He is an artist who creates art for its own sake.

He says that he is inspired by me because I have lived through such adversity and am still happy, well-balanced and alive... He never ever ridicules or humiliates me.

In a Spirit Mates relationship, or at least in ours, there is never a need to manipulate the other to get satisfaction. If we want or need something, we ask. No relationship can work entirely telepathically (although we are quite good at that too!), so we talk a lot about what we want and have found that this creates safety for us both. This does not mean, however, that we bang on endlessly about our relationship, but just that we know what the other feels and thinks. These discussions are generally brief, never accusatory and they reestablish balance immediately.

Of course, we do not agree on every single thing but I would say that we agree on 99 percent of things. We have never argued about money, politics or differing world-views. If we do not agree about something (domestic or otherwise) we tend to have a mutually curious discussion. I, however, am much more likely to want to go into the deepest aspects of things whereas François will ponder as he works and report back later. We are both allergic to drama and therefore try to create the most peaceful, creative, free and loving environment possible. If external drama intrudes on our energetic space then we shut it right down as quickly as possible. We are so highly tuned into each other that any slight modification in energy is immediately apparent and we take rapid action to restore balance. François is highly sensitive to criticism and I am very direct when I have something to say but we both feel that clear communication is a new and positive element that we did not have in past relationships.

Being in a Spirit Mates couple feels absolutely natural. It is a place of safety that does not fear change. It is a place from which each individual is free to explore any avenue of life knowing that said exploration will benefit and strengthen the couple. It is a place where you can reveal every aspect of yourself, knowing that the other person will welcome whatever it may be. There is no competitiveness in such a relationship, as both parties stand to gain so much from the expansion of the other.

Both François and I have lived through a lot of difficulties in one way or another. We have both, at various times encountered overwhelming resistance on our respective paths and this has helped us both to know that what we are fortunate to have is worth protecting. It strengthens us, it gives us an even greater sense of belonging. After traveling for work (him or me) the moment we are reunited is always both powerful and comforting. We belong together, everybody can see it.

Neither of us would advocate cutting off a finger in order to attract your Spirit Mate's attention but know that your Spirit energy might just create an incident to kick you into the realization that your "other half" is not the stuff of wild dreams and that he or she is longing to meet you too.

What happens when your Spirit Mate dies?

We have decided that we don't want to dig too deep into this very sad topic, since the thought of losing your one and only spiritual love partner is almost impossible to think through for the human brain, because the brain cannot think in terms of spirit in a logical way. Spirit can only be sensed through intuition in the body and aura.

Most Spirit Mates cannot imagine how life is going to be without the other half of their own energy being physically present in their daily life, and especially not if they have had the pleasure of living together as a physical love couple. Because how can you separate yourself from yourself, which is exactly how it feels when you try to separate a Spirit Mates couple from each other? And how can you take away the most natural part from your life and replace it with pure spirit energy, where you are forced to communicate with your love partner through spirit instead of having a wonderful human and earthly conversation with each other?

When your love partner dies there is no longer a physical and human energy to relate to in daily life, which can make most people go crazy. Furthermore, it doesn't feel natural to suddenly feel your deceased love partner communicating through your own body. So of course, people who have already met their Spirit Mate don't want to replace their existing physical love partner with a more high-frequency Spirit Mate with a much higher vibration that matches the existing Spirit Mates couple's united energy, just to develop even further on a spiritual level.

Most people on Earth with a good grounding would never want such things to happen just to be able to raise their level of spirit. Instead, they would prefer that the energy upgrade took place in between their earthly lives and not while they are alive in a physical body.

In the next love story, Eva from Sweden shares with you what happened when she lost Peter as her Spirit Mate on a physical level and melted together with him on a spiritual level. Please don't cry too much and try to see the beauty in the unique love transformation process that most of us would never want to experience in our physical lives.

After Peter died, Anni gave Eva this very essential and useful advice, because Eva felt that certain people around her responded to Peter's energy in her by being angry at her. Apparently, they felt that Peter's energy was in the wrong place, and that Eva had taken it. Peter's energy in Eva simply reminded them that he was gone, and when they looked at her, they saw his energy in her and got angry at her instead of him for leaving too soon, even if she missed him as much as they did.

"Gather all your own energy and Peter's energy in one big energy pool in you. Then other people will not recognize Peter's energy in you and you will not be blamed for his early death. Then you will hopefully feel more whole and peaceful inside!"

Eva and Peter

Text in the photo: Sleep well, my beloved Peter

Love Story # 9

A beautiful fairy tale that ended!

Eva: Peter and I lived a parallel life since I was about 20 years old and Peter 25 years old, but we met and spoke for the first time in June of 2005. We had done similar things in our lives and we had many common friends. We met at a spiritual workshop where he came up to me and asked if I was his relative, because I looked a lot like his aunts. We found out that we were second cousins.

We began to see each other and it was always very easy and interesting to talk to Peter; he was someone special to me and I quickly fell in love with him. I wrote a letter that I gave to him where I explained my feelings. I told him that I loved him for the person he was, and not because of his appearance, which he was accustomed to when it came to other girls. Peter called me that evening; he was very polite and said he was interested in someone else. I also knew that he liked very slim girls – which I wasn't.

We continued to see each other and we were very good friends at the same time that we both had other relationships that we didn't feel good in. We talked a lot about our relationships and how we reacted to the problems in them.

We had a lot in common in that we both loved to travel on "backpacker trips," and we were both very freedom-loving people. We enjoyed sitting and talking about "deep things" such as what's happening in the world. We both wanted to become better people. I felt I had met someone like myself who also was a little odd, that had very deep thoughts, and that I could even laugh together with.

At the end of July 2011, I did my AuraTransformation™ and two months after that Peter asked me if I wanted to be his girlfriend. I was shocked because I had stopped believing that he wanted to have a relationship with me; I knew that I wasn't his type.

The weekend after we decided to be a couple, we went to my friend Teresaa, who is an Aura Mediator™, and Peter also did his AuraTransformation™.

I knew when he came out that something had changed in his energy. The most amazing feeling was when I lay in his arms because I felt like we fused together and had the same energy frequency; energetically we became one. Everything around me disappeared and I felt so calm and happy to just lie in his arms while we both actually were two restless people. We could lie like that or just talk for hours; it seemed as if we never had enough time because there was so much to talk about. I felt that he understood me as no one else had done before, and I felt so safe in his presence.

Peter had left my letter in his backpack, which he always carried with him everywhere, and the strange thing was that six months after we had become a couple he lost it somewhere and we never found it again.

When I read the book "Spirit Mates – The New Time Relationship" that Anni and Carsten wrote, I realized that much of what I was reading was exactly what we had in our relationship. Anni was the person who confirmed that we were Spirit Mates. The reason everything wasn't quite clear to us I realized afterwards, when I could see the common thread:

Peter wouldn't stay here on Earth. We met and had an extremely intense and challenging period in our lives for 5 years. Peter had had a very difficult and tragic childhood; he had been through so much in his life. That was a major reason that he developed alcoholism – he became a binge drinker. When I met Peter he was in the midst of his 8-year-long period of sobriety. He had traveled around a lot and he had owned two big companies and been very rich, which didn't make him happy as he put it. He lived in all extremes and wanted to experience everything. He was a very wise man who had learned a lot during his lifetime, much due to his alcoholism as he earnestly worked with the 12-step program. He was a very open person who wanted to find out everything about himself. He was a musician and a creative person, but he found it hard to be happy for longer periods. He sometimes saw all too clearly what happened in the world and it depressed him. He had many ups and downs in his life and he had treated his body in the same way. He had sometimes both mental and physical problems despite the fact that he ate very healthy and exercised a lot. The biggest problem was that he couldn't sleep, so in the end he lost his life spark. He died in Greece in October of 2016 from an aneurysm.

When I met Anni Sennov at a workshop in Falkenberg, Sweden two weeks before Peter's death, she could see that I had two different energies in my aura and body as she told me afterwards. She saw my and another person's energy that had gathered into a dual energy in me, but she couldn't see who the other energy belonged to. Only when Peter died a few weeks later, did she understand that she, at the workshop, had seen the initial fusion between Peter's and my energies. This fusion was completed after his death, when I felt his spirit had completely left the Earth.

Peter and I had long periods of immense happiness and satisfaction just being with each other; for the first time in my life I loved a man totally without reservation. I felt that I could feel every cell in his body and he in mine. We were completely honest with each other and we talked about everything in a constructive and stimulating way and we grew tremendously in this relationship. It was such a beautiful love story that we shared, even if sometimes we had it tough because of his moods. We both found the partner we had always been searching for; there were no requirements on how the other would be or act. He always said that if we can't live together I would rather live alone because I'll never find someone like you. You are my guitar in my guitar case (he played guitar and bass). Other women may be beautiful but there is no one who can replace you.

We never fought but there could be discussions where we became irritated, but that was also rare. We were both spiritual people with that kind of thinking, and we always treated each other with great respect.

I miss him terribly physically, although I know that we have fused together as one spirit now. I could feel his energy come into my body a few hours after he had died. I have lost my best friend and my security in life and I have to adapt myself to that now. Peter was the most beautiful person I have ever met and the void is enormous!

I can see some advantages to us having fused together as one spirit, and that is that I can finally use Peter's determination, in order to lose weight and take care of my body. I also think that I see things more clearly now, but often I don't recognize my reactions in my body. Sometimes I get confused about what is happening and I have, for example, difficulty eating nutritional supplements as I get shaky from them, as Peter reacted when he had his insomnia. I guess everything will be integrated in due course and that I will be whole in the new way that is my new me.

I hope that something good will come out of this and that, with time, I will be able to see my growing as a spirit, more than the pain over losing Peter.

From what I understand I will probably find a new Spirit Mate, and it can be even better than how it was with Peter; so that feels wonderful. I long to continue to grow together with my new Spirit Mate and long to feel whole again, to continue my development in this life on Earth, when I look at it from a higher perspective.

Can you melt together too much?

Eva and Peter's love story was complicated at times because Peter didn't feel completely at home in the physical world. However, when he was together with Eva he felt more grounded and quite human, which makes it easier for most of us to accept the fact that when they are now together as two compatible energies in Eva's body, Peter's energy will be much more grounded than it was before. This is of course a somewhat surrealistic way of thinking, but spiritual energy isn't always logical seen from a human perspective.

It is inevitable that a Spirit Mate will die at some point in time, since no human on Planet Earth can expect to life forever. Therefore, you may want to know more about what happens when one Spirit Mate passes away, but we have decided to not focus much on that topic in this book.

You may also want to know more about what happened in Eva's life after Peter died and how their energies were united even more, but we kindly ask you to use your own imagination to figure out how things are supposed to develop in a Spirit Mates relationship when it's time for the love couple to melt their energies into one big energy pool being placed in only one body instead of two bodies.

We cannot tell you if this sad experience could have been prevented, because we honestly don't know. Instead, we recommend that you consult God and your highest spiritual source to get the answer, which may not be the same in all situations, simply because all living beings are different from each other and we all have our own unique dharma and life purpose.

However, if you want to know if it is possible for Spirit Mates to melt their energies together too much in daily life, the answer is "YES!" That we know all about from our own love relationship, and from our clients and other people.

If Spirit Mates are about to get too close to each other's energies they will usually have to separate their energies or themselves from each other in one way or another. Otherwise, the result will be that one person will have lots of energy while the other is lacking energy. This is because there is no personal balance in the couple's mutual spiritual energy, if they have only focused on the spiritual part and not the personal part.

So, if a Spirit Mates love couple wants to raise the overall energy level in their relationship and they don't tell the spirit energy that this is not supposed to be the final gathering of their energies, they risk melting together at a much higher spiritual level in only one body with only one person being able to benefit from the united energy, just like what happened to Eva and Peter.

A separation phase is therefore needed to lower the frequency level in both bodies, so the couple consisting of two strong energy personalities can land on the ground and be visible to the surrounding world in a way that most people can relate to in daily life.

If Spirit Mates melt together their common energy in all aspects of life, they might as well be relatives and "just" love each other with no specific passion or physical attraction between them, because that is what happens to Spirit Mates when they unite their energies 100%. Then they become one and the same energy in two different bodies and no one around them can relate to such a compressed human energy setup.

Uniting your energies 100% in the relationship is exactly what most Spirit Mates love couples long to do when having sex together, and it is for sure possible to get this unique sense of unity that you cannot have with anybody else. Especially at the beginning of the relationship.

At a later stage in the relationship the couple has gained so much trust in each other that they don't want to be in control of their partner's energy in any way. Instead, they prefer to go with the flow and see what comes to the surface when being together, and thereby welcome all new adventures and initiatives that both parties come up with for the benefit of the couple. Therefore, they don't try to be in charge of their partner's energy on an unconscious level to get closer to him/her, because then they will never be able to be happily surprised by their love partner.

If you and your Spirit Mate are 100% connected in spirit on a human level and you have full access to each other's minds and thoughts, you cannot be surprised by each other like most other love couples. Therefore, some of the attraction might be lost because you know your partner's inner wishes, personal needs and thoughts so well as if they were your own. So instead of searching for excitement outside of the relationship to create excitement in your love relationship, you should try to separate your energies a bit more in your relationship by being together with different types of people on a regular basis to be extraordinarily inspired or by being away from each other for a couple of days when traveling with work or playing sports, etc.

This is one sure way to create more attraction in a Spirit Mates relationship if you have melted together your energies too much and have become so much alike that the attraction between you is about to disappear in everyday life.

Your common life task

All Spirit Mates couples have a common mission in life, which they are expected to fulfill during their earthly relationship with each other. The fulfillment of their precise overall life purpose is actually the main reason that Spirit Mates get to meet each other and to live together on Planet Earth.

The second reason for the love couple to meet is for them to be able to live through a high vibration of love in daily life, which ensures that everything they do, feel, think and say is always mediating the high vibration of love that they feel for each other to the surrounding world.

The actual results of this life goal are not predetermined, and neither is the path that the Spirit Mates couple is expected to move along together, in order to realize their common life purpose.

The person in the Spirit Mates relationship with the strongest earthly connection from the outset, may easily have sensed their common life mission deep inside many years before the couple was able to meet, where it has remained as a kind of future coding in the consciousness.

The other partner, who would most often have had a more conscious spiritual approach to life, will instead have seen their life task as a vision that they were expected to live out sometime in the future.

In order for Spirit Mates to identify their common great mission in life, there are some phases in their relationship that they must first pass through:

1. The couple has to choose each other as love partners.

2. Then, and often fairly quickly, they will together create a framework for everyday life and a joint physical platform in the outer world, corresponding to the consciousness standpoint they have together on the spirit level. This provides peace and security in the relationship and daily life.

3. As a key factor in the joint mission being revealed to them, the Spirit Mates couple must go through a stage in the relationship where they open their hearts completely to each other so that they can fully unite with their cores and their common life purpose, which is hidden deep within both of their hearts.

   Only with love and by opening both hearts simultaneously and collectively will their common life purpose present itself, so that the realization of their goal in life can begin in the outer world.

The path to your Spirit Mate

Even if you have not yet met your Spirit Mate in physical life, you can do something yourself to accelerate this connection on the spirit level, and in this way create the basis for an earlier meeting with your one and only.

However, it is important to keep in mind that your Spirit Mate will not just pop up in your life simply because you send a request to God that you want the person to be sent to you at once. Selfish actions are not rewarded. They are actually a sign that you are not yet pure in your consciousness, and therefore not ready to be joined with your Spirit Mate yet. Moreover, it is not certain that your Spirit Mate is ready to meet you on a personal level, which may cause more trouble and disappointment in the relationship than you have ever dreamt about, because you couldn't wait for things to happen at the right time.

It is your inner intentions and consciousness level that are assessed when it is time to be joined with your Spirit Mate so that you can both embark on a new era of consciousness in life. Attracting your Spirit Mate has basically nothing to do with what you want on a personal level. It's all about creating spiritual synchronization between you as a couple so that together you can manifest your common life purpose and dharma on a much higher level than when you do it alone.

So, when you finally meet your Spirit Mate in real life, you feel rewarded and it creates the basis for a whole new balance between what you give to others and what you get back, and this will make you want to contribute even more to make this world a better place for all people. Besides that, meeting your Spirit Mate will of course give you great personal pleasure and enjoyment.

The first step on the path is to find balance within yourself. This is done through self-development and can be helped by various personal development and boundary-stretching courses, etc.

You have to follow your own way through the personality-development jungle by constantly tuning into your heart and listening in order to find the right answer for you. You will have no joy from walking paths recommended by others if they do not feel right for you. However, we can definitely recommend that you get an AuraTransformation™ as part of your personal development. With an AuraTransformation™ you will have the New Time spirit-based consciousness structure integrated into your aura, which makes it possible for you to meet on an equal level with your Spirit Mate. However, this does not mean that you will then automatically meet your Spirit Mate and that your Spirit Mate has already had an AuraTransformation™ and upgrade of his/her aura structure.

As most Spirit Mates often develop synchronously on a personal and spiritual level before they meet as love partners in real life, your Spirit Mate might be inspired to also upgrade their personal energy and aura structure because they can sense through the air that you have made a life-changing decision that will move you away from the consciousness level at which they are usually located in daily life. So suddenly, they feel an inner urge to also make big changes in their life.

AuraTransformation™ is a significant step on the path to meeting this person in real life here on Earth, and it will help in many ways to speed up your personal development process considerably.

The next step in your personal development path follows when you feel that you are in complete balance with yourself. Then you can send out the following thought:

**"Where are you my Spirit Mate?
I am ready to meet you!"**

This thought consists of two elements. It is both a request, as well as an ultimate message that you are ready to meet your one and only.

Sending out the thought can take place anytime and anywhere. Then God, Planet Earth and the overall consciousness in the Universe will do the rest when the time is right. However, you can amplify the power of the message if you mobilize all your energy when you send out the thought.

Your Spirit Mate will unconsciously pick up the signal, as this will act as an inner voice that calls to him or her. The further your Spirit Mate has advanced in their personal development towards inner balance, the sooner you will meet each other. Your call will get your Spirit Mate to unconsciously speed up their own development process in order to get into balance more quickly and be ready to meet you. The deep-seated longing to meet their one and only that everyone has inside them will now come to the surface and get your Spirit Mate to further accelerate their consciousness development.

In this way the Universe will bring you together when you are both ready and in place in your own energies.

As you may have noticed from the stories shared in this book, there do not need to be any big sparks between you at your first meeting, as there probably needs to be some fine-tuning between you. This is work that goes on behind-the-scenes and is not always visible to the Spirit Mates themselves. However, the couple will quickly detect a mutual recognition and a feeling of equality, and from there things will speed up by themselves.

All you have to do is take action and follow the flow and then you will experience the ultimate love and a feeling of ease in the relationship.

When your Soul Mate and your Spirit Mate is the same

Meeting as a love couple at soul level creates an opportunity for both of you to also be love partners at spirit level. In most cases, however, it feels like being together with two very different love partners instead of being with one and the same person at different times in life. First you connect at soul level and later on at spirit level, and for some reason all memories of your past at soul level will be gone when you upgrade to spirit level. It's only when you look at photos, and other people talk about the past, that you can see and sense the big difference between before and after the entrance of pure spirit energy in your lives.

It may sound exciting, but it can be extremely challenging for any relationship to start all over on a totally new consciousness platform. In most cases it feels like you must ask all the same questions again that you already asked each other back in time, because everything between you has changed so much that you cannot just rely on whatever you thought and knew back then.

Your love partner may be in the process of changing their view of life so much that nothing is ever going to be the same again, or maybe he/she will suddenly change their life view overnight because they've had a clear vision that made so much sense to them, and that opened their mind to a higher consciousness level. Such an energy expansion will of course influence you and affect your life in all areas, so you have to think things through to decide whether it is something that you can also support and relate to. Therefore, it can take a long time for you as a love couple to touch base, share your thoughts and ideas, and to meet on a new common ground.

The deep foundation of being a Spirit Mates couple is unconditional love and support for each other. At the same time, it is very important that each of you are in charge of your own energy, so that you are not being controlled by the energy of others, not even your love partner. Fulfilling your common life purpose requires that both of you are aligned on a personal level as well as energy-wise, because it's both of you who are on a spiritual mission, not your energies. However, your energies have to be in balance at all levels before you can accomplish your common mission.

In the following love story, you can read about Susanne and Antti from Finland who met each other at soul level, where things changed radically when they had their respective energies upgraded to spirit level via an AuraTransformation™. You could say that they have lived two different lives with the same love partner who was actually not the exact same person energy-wise, because of the radical energy shift they both went through on a consciousness level.

Love is the foundation of their relationship as well as an inspiration, and major challenges in the relationship have made it possible for the couple to support and love each other unconditionally. They just know that they belong together no matter what, and that nothing can ever separate them from each other.

Susanne and Antti are two people on a mission. They each have their own mission, but they also have a common mission in life, their Family Earth project. So when reading their love story you will get a very clear feeling of how it is to work closely together with your Spirit Mate to fulfill your common dharma, and how you support each other in different ways that are not always visible to others.

Susanne and Antti

Love Story # 10

Susanne: Tattoos. Of everything that could have brought us together, it was tattoos that were the merging link. I have always been fascinated by them and knew at an early age that I would get a tattoo myself as soon as I could. I have, for as long as I can remember, seen them as beautiful and I have been attracted by their characteristics. A tattoo can be an image, but it can also be a symbol and a story. The interest grew for Antti in his teens, as since he was a child he had loved to draw, and when he got a little older, he thought tattoos were the coolest way you could draw.

Antti: When I was young, I felt that things just "happened" without me being able to or having the knowledge to influence them. Especially when it came to couple relationships. I concentrated mostly on doing my best regarding my studies and my art, and even if it was easy for me to make friends/acquaintances, couple relationships were something that didn't work so easily for me. When it came to them I didn't understand what was expected of me. I didn't search consciously for anyone, but rather had a desire to not have to be alone. But I didn't know specifically what I should do about that desire.

When I later met Sussi (Susanne), my start-up company was taking up all my waking hours. Of course, I saw her the first time she came into my workplace. I tried to carefully concentrate on tattooing a client at the same time that everything about her drew my attention away from the work I was doing. I was overjoyed when she wanted to schedule an appointment for a tattoo with me and I nearly counted the days until I could get to know her better. I realized quickly that I wanted to spend as much time as possible with her. I was very insecure and nervous, but I knew I wanted to be together, as much as I could be with her. According to me, she was (and still is) the most beautiful woman I've ever seen.

Susanne: The first time we met (in 2002) was when I went into Antti's tattoo studio. I wasn't at all prepared or ready to meet the person who would turn out to be the man in my life. But when I stepped through the door and saw him where he sat and tattooed, it was like all the cells in my whole existence jumped up. It was also a feeling that I had never experienced before, and even though I reacted as I did, it was still a very calm and safe experience. I remember that I thought quietly to myself: "Aah, so this is where you are." It felt like coming home, that I found the person I unconsciously (and also consciously) longed for and sought after. It was an experience that I never before experienced and it also, of course, didn't hurt that he was irresistibly attractive.

It took a while before we became a couple and I can honestly say that I did what I could to capture his interest. In retrospect, it's a little funny because he had seen me that first time and had thought that he would never have a chance to be with me. But thanks to our youth and shyness, neither of us dared to say anything, which resulted in that we were like two cats around a plate of hot porridge until we finally worked up the courage and told it like it was. The feeling when we met was electric, as it can be when you have just fallen in love, but I felt that this was something more. It felt like a solid ground to stand on, a home that we would build together, and a security where we could rest and gather energy. A foundation from which we could grow both together and as individuals.

The path that led us to where we are today

Susanne: For me, the spiritual world has always been with me, ever since I was a small child, but for Antti it was a foreign world. Despite the fact that he was open from the first moment to that side of me, and instead of trying to diminish or ridicule it (which I had previously experienced, and not just in couple relationships), he encouraged me to become the person I had really always been. He was, therefore, also very supportive when I told him that I had come in contact with a treatment that I intuitively felt that I needed and would do. I remember that it felt incredibly liberating to not have to explain or defend who I was and what was important to me. He was and still is the man who really understands me and knows me best and Antti experiences the same with me. We don't even always use words; we know where we have each other. It was a very nice feeling when we discovered and realized that we could trust each other 100%. The treatment that I felt was so important was the AuraTransformation™. Neither of us had gone through it when we met and later even became a couple. We were actually together for years before we came in contact with the treatment form, and it was I who first did mine in 2012 and Antti then did his in 2013.

Seen in retrospect, it's almost like seeing two different relationships, one before and one that came after the AuraTransformation™. We had a good relationship before which was based on love, respect and trust for each other, but we had our individual anchors that slowed us and occasionally pulled us down. For me it resulted in a huge life crisis and disease that took several years from my life, years that are still partially erased from my memory. For Antti it resulted in a sense of frustration and a standstill on his personal life path. He was aware that he carried a lot more potential than what he currently had the space and capacity to realize. We had quite honestly some very tough years where it was more about trying to survive than enjoying life and being happy to live. We are still genuinely grateful also for just those years because without them we wouldn't even be a fraction of what and who we are today. Although it was a question of difficult moments, both physically and mentally, we learned a tremendous amount on many different levels from that period in our lives. After we took ourselves out of these dark years, we know that we are always there for each other. We are absolutely clear that we want to live and that we want to do it together.

Antti: Fairly quickly after we became a couple Sussi became ill. It feels difficult, almost impossible, to remember those years and also how I was as a person before it. It feels like there's a wide wall from the time we were newly in love to when it slowly but surely began to look brighter for her strength and health. We went through a lot during that time. For me it was extremely difficult to simply stand next to the person I love so much and not really be able to help. It was a heavy and frustrating time for both of us and it happened that I even got comments from outsiders that perhaps it would be best if we went our separate ways. Those comments made me mad. Why would we leave each other just because we were in a difficult situation? We loved each other and despite all the hardships, there was a seed of hope, perhaps even a knowing, that it would get better for us. Today, I am pleased that we could get through that time and I know that it has brought with it important things for both of us.

Susanne: For me the AuraTransformation™ came as a gift I had waited a long time for, and after I completed the treatment life started to fall into place in a way I hadn't thought was possible. Everything began to happen faster and my life path became so much clearer. That which previously was like a thin, and at times barely audible, whisper inside became a clear voice, namely my own inner voice and truth. Of course, this also affected our relationship and both Antti and I experienced that I rushed forward at a faster pace than he had the ability for. It became clear to me what I should do with my life and I came in contact with my life tasks in a tangible manner; something that I previously just had a feeling about, but I had found difficult to grasp onto. This included becoming an Aura Mediator™. The whole time Antti was there beside me supporting me and allowing me to get in touch with who I was. Barely a year after I completed my AuraTransformation™ Antti felt that it was also time for him to do his, and we both experienced that it was natural that I should be his Aura Mediator™. For him the treatment felt like landing and that a calm and strength spread inside of him. It became easier for him to see where he wanted to lay his energy and how he should use his energy. There was, in other words, a noticeable difference after we both had completely risen into our life paths, and now our shared path was starting to be made visible to us. In the past we had both, at least in part, felt our life tasks and imagined a vision far away on the horizon of what could be a shared path as well as a task. That vision was made clear and we could start to see and know which way we should go, when we should wait, and what it was that we were traveling towards. We knew that our shared task lay ahead of us, but that we weren't ready for it yet, and we also knew that we were heading towards something that was very important to us.

So it is an understatement to say that both our relationship and our individual personal development really got a boost thanks to the process. After we stood in our own energy and we had landed in our physical bodies as well as in our energy, our relationship became so much more than what it had been before. As time went on, the original security and love grew deeper and deeper, and we felt that we fused together and became a shared existence, without losing our own identity and personal truth and reality. This was clearly a very interesting discovery, and nothing that either of us had experienced before.

If you who are reading this haven't been through anything like this, maybe you can imagine the feeling of first landing completely in who you have been, in who you are and who you can be. This allows you to clean out and remove anything that is no longer able to bring something to you and your life. It allows you to strengthen and rebuild what is important to you, and you yourself choose what tools and materials you want to use. The possibilities are endless and just that is hugely inspiring! Then you will also see how the person closest to you goes through the same process. Finally, you have time to catch up with each other and can begin to grow together, learn together and look at your shared life and where you want to go.

The love that is in all of this is a love that is hard to describe. It's a love that exists; it's available as a base, a foundation, and at the same time it exists as an inspiration and a promise to always be there. For us it's a calm feeling, a feeling that we know is always there for us and that we have no need to proclaim or make it either smaller or larger than what it is. We just know that we love each other, that we belong together and that we want to live together.

What is it like being Spirit Mates?

When we compare our relationship with previous relationships we feel that we lie very far from what we shared with previous partners. We balance each other out very well and at the same time we can push and encourage each other to grow, to dare to challenge ourselves and to want to live life in our way. We enjoy each other's company and we are each other's best friends. It feels like we belong together and it's a very natural feeling.

In previous situations, there has, in one way or another, always been some form of insecurity and lack of security in the background. There hasn't been the possibility to be fully able to relax or to be ourselves, and no opportunity to really get to know the other person. Early on, when we became a couple, it felt like we could relax and trust each other. A purely practical example is that we don't argue the same way we have done in previous relationships. Of course we have discussions, but that's also what they are; we discuss and talk instead of shouting and arguing with each other. We want to reach a solution together and we want the solution to be in balance with us both. Jealousy is also another thing that we feel is completely different in our relationship than in previous relationships. Since we have this sturdy platform on which we stand there is just no room for jealousy.

That we are Spirit Mates wasn't something we had words for, or thought about, before we came into contact with the concept. But once we did, it felt like an understandable and true description of what we had and still have. But we also want to highlight, as well as be clear about, that even though we are Spirit Mates we still have our challenges, both as a couple and as individuals. There will be moments when we can be really irritated; not everything is a delightful dance 24/7. We are human beings and we aren't perfect. What is crucial, and which means we don't have to explode (as we have done in previous relationships), is that we know where we have ourselves and we have each other. We can be secure in our feelings and in our inner truth. We share a common sense and a common objective and we rely completely on one another. For us it has definitely been a liberating experience to make room for each other and for ourselves in all of life's swings.

Something that is a common factor for both of us is that we love to learn and to grow. To be creative and to create is our *Air*. That feeling permeates our relationship and, of course, there is a feeling that moves us forward. By us having this shared part, we also have something that contributes constructively to our life. Before we met, we couldn't think as holistically as we can today, and we also lacked the ability to concretize and materialize in the way that we now can. As we move further along our path, our elements have, of course, also developed and we with them. Along the way, we have balanced each other on many different levels, and for us it has been a great help that we have gotten to know our elements: Fire, Water, Earth and Air. Thanks to us doing that, we have access to more powerful tools that we can use not only in our professional lives, but also in our personal life. Our interest and our drive to learn, as well as our feeling and the desire to contribute to a better world are all things that began to look differently after we met. The main difference above all is that these parts are visible to us now, as opposed to before we were together. When we look in the rearview mirror, we see that a lot has really happened since we met, so you could almost say that we have lived several lives since 2002. It's fascinating how couples can find so many parts of themselves and each other. It's a lottery win that we found each other and we really wish that those of you reading this (if you haven't already), also win the lottery. Our spiritual and earthly development have brought so much to our lives, and we are confident that we could never have gotten to where we are today if A) we had not met, and B) we had not been in contact with Anni and Carsten Sennov's work.

The absolutely greatest difference from *before* we met to *after* we met is that since we became a couple, we have found security within ourselves and each other. In addition, we have also found a joy and curiosity for all of life's possibilities. It's rewarding and uplifting to live together and to share such a warm love, a love that is difficult to describe with words. The closeness we share together is a harmonious feeling, while it's also a force that gives us energy. For Susanne, Antti is the most beautiful human being in existence and for Antti, Susanne is the most beautiful human being in existence. The attraction that we have for each other lies on several levels;

mentally and physically. All that we share, and everything that we do together, adds something to our life. We aren't bored together, we always have something interesting to talk about and we have fun together. Today we are more ourselves than we have been and we have a strong belief in our life as it is and as it will be. We are simply more stable in our lives since we met.

Specifically, this means that

- we live in our dream home, which is a pretty small but picturesque cottage in the country;

- we have a close relationship with the landscape and nature, and we nourish this relationship by being out in nature as often as possible;

- we have our own little family flock of animals that we love above everything else;

- we have realized ourselves on the individual level, among other things, by developing our abilities purely professionally; and

- we have begun work on our shared life mission.

These things, or maybe some of them, may seem small to some people but to us they are hugely important pieces of the puzzle. Before we met, we lay in the collective mind loop of how life should be and what we were expected to do. Something which we today regard as a rather limited way of life. We have gotten out of that loop and that means, among other things, that we left behind those expectations we had in life before we met. We are no longer interested in living in a big house, making a career or having to mold ourselves into the normal and expected family picture. We want to live our way.

What does it mean to live our way? One of the major pieces of the puzzle was that neither of us wanted to have children. It has never been an issue, a problem for us; we made a conscious choice not to have children early in our relationship. That puzzle piece might make some of you raise an eyebrow, but that's how we feel and think.

Susanne: Right from childhood, I have always liked animals, and for most of my life I preferred to spend time with animals rather than with humans. (Something my AuraTransformation™ helped me with; so today I can relax and enjoy human companionship too.) But since I, for as long as I can remember, had such a strong feeling for animals, it was also natural that I relate faster and easier to them. I simply haven't had any interest in being a parent.

For Antti the question of having children hasn't been something important; he hasn't felt that being a dad is his mission. After we met, his relationship with animals and nature also began to grow and it has led him to feel a strong connection with them.

So we chose in a very undramatic way not to raise a family, at least not in the traditional way. We both relate more to animals and to nature, and this has resulted in that we are now a family pack with five members, and we feel as much at home in our small house as when we spend time in nature. On our daily walks in the forest, together with our beloved boys (poodle guys Ivar, Arwid and Oskar), we enjoy contact with Mother Earth. In other words, one can say that for us, the animals are our family and nature is our home. If we weren't Spirit Mates, this would hardly have worked and this puzzle piece wouldn't have fallen so smoothly into place. What a gift it is to find your other half and to be able to feel how smooth a relationship can actually be...

When we were going to get married, the decision fell on how we could make that be just as smooth. We immediately agreed that we wanted a very small, intimate ceremony in the woods under our favorite tree with Ivar, Arwid and Oskar. We wanted to get married just as we are, in our usual forest clothes and without a lot of frills. We chose to have the actual wedding reception a few months later, and it was a celebration that we wanted to share with our loved ones. But the ceremony, when we said yes to each other, we wanted to keep for ourselves, where our hearts find peace and we can recharge our energy. To have our dear boys with us was a given and their presence made the whole experience even more complete. Something that helped even more to brighten the moment was an eagle that flew over us when we said yes to each other, and we looked up at the top of our favorite tree. It was a magical moment. We never encountered any accusatory faces or a questioning of our choice from our extended family members, and they expressed no feelings of being excluded. On the contrary, we were instead supported and understood, something we see as signs of love and a natural acceptance.

Our family's reaction to our decision on how we would get married is also a pretty good summary of how most people have responded to our relationship. In other words, undramatic. We have been told how we are "kultapari" which is Finnish and means something like the perfect couple. For ourselves, we don't think we are the perfect couple and we have no desire to be one, we just wish and hope to live together and share all of life's possibilities.

Our shared life task

We have our separate professional lives. Antti is a recognized talented tattoo artist and visual artist, and Susanne has a long experience of working with energy and well-being with both people and animals. Through the years, we haven't only grown in our professional roles, but also in our knowledge, as well as in the way we work. Even here we have had the great joy of the foundation that our relationship gives us, and this means that we not only have had interest, but also opportunity to develop our individual touches. Despite the fact that we seem to work on completely different things, our professional lives are woven together, and that's because we share a vision and a drive to help and create. Creativity is really one of our shared interests and we are both fascinated by art in different forms. For Susanne it's definitely something that has grown since we became a couple. She had never painted a picture before, but thanks to Antti and how he inspired her, she began one day to suddenly paint and today several of her paintings have found their homes around Finland. So this is yet another concrete example of how she's grown together with him. For Antti it's instead his spirituality, as well as his connection to nature and animals, that has deepened since we got together. We also love to discover the world together by traveling and at the same time discovering what it means to live. For us, life is so much more fulfilling today than it was before we met each other.

One of the greatest common denominators for us is the love and contact with animals and nature. We care about well-being and balance when it comes to all forms of life, no matter how many bones (or if there are none at all) there are. So it's perhaps not so surprising that our shared task also has to do with just that; well-being and balance for all forms of life. It took a while before our task became fully clear and tangible for us. From the time we saw it on the energetic level until it materialized, took about 3 years. The reason why it took so long was because it was *necessary*. Our energy systems and bodies needed to first fully integrate the energy that lies in and around our life mission. During the process, we were treated to a variety of insights of different intensity. The easiest way to describe it is as if we were pregnant. It was namely how it felt; both in our energy and in our bodies. It started with us carrying what came to us, then the task needed to lie and mature, as well as grow within us. When our energy systems had carried the task as long as was needed, it was time to release it and let it come forward into the world. It was fascinating to go through this together, to feel that we together were on our way towards something, and to feel how this something grew stronger and clearer as time went by. It was an experience that once again brought us even closer together. When it was finally time for us to release our shared project out into the world, we both felt that we were virtually ready to burst.

What we had worked to bring forward and realize was what today is known as Family Earth™. Family Earth™ is a nonprofit organization, a network and a community for people who work with restoring the balance between animals, nature and humanity. Our wish is to inspire people to live in balance with our planet, with our home. We want to help people get in touch with themselves and with the Earth's life.

Family Earth™ is an organization that stretches from the spiritual to the physical and the Earth. With our work we want to, among other things, build bridges and help increase understanding of life in all its forms. We believe in cooperation and that we can all do something, contribute in some way, to help. It begins with our daily actions and choices; each of us determine what kind of rings we want to spread on the water. It's no longer possible to live without taking responsibility for our lives and at the same time expect that what you choose to do (or to not do) isn't relevant to our environment. We have gone past the point where we can live and simply do as we have always done. Every choice and action bring us forward in our lives, and with our life we can choose to either contribute to a better world or hand over responsibility to someone else. The problem is only **who** is this someone else?

Who has the responsibility and the task of cleaning up after our failures or for taking care of what we haven't wanted to take care of? If we, as adults, don't do everything we can to steer the ship, today's youth and children will have to put on the dust coat, right? And it is not a small dust coat that will need to be worn... It is, among other things, here that Family Earth™ would like to contribute with what we can. For us the focus is on what is possible, not what is impossible.

The work with Family Earth™ is, of course, hugely important to us. We have a strong belief in everyone's strength and ability and we feel strongly about life in all its forms. We believe in building up and strengthening the positive and constructive. We know that all individuals carry something unique and beautiful that actually is a gift of Life in its entirety. Everyone is needed and everyone can do something to create a world and a reality that is in tune with what is possible. With Family Earth™ we hope to be able to help where we can and inspire others to do the same. Our work is all about teamwork: teamwork for our home, for Mother Earth.

How do you find your Spirit Mate?

The advice we give to those who want to find their Spirit Mate can seem both simple and difficult; you find your Spirit Mate by not looking. Frustrating, isn't it? The reason we want to give that tip is that we ourselves have experienced (and have seen others undergo a similar process) what it means to look for something when you may not even know what it is you are looking for until you are ready to face it. Then the search in itself risks slowing down the possibility of finding who/what you are looking for. We found each other when we were ready. We both needed go our separate ways before we could become a couple, and we had to learn different things and experience life without each other before we got together. By doing that, we prepared ourselves to meet.

But having said that, you can of course facilitate your process of finding your Spirit Mate and you do that, first of all, by taking care of yourself. Help yourself feel as good as possible and try to be patient and trust that you too will find your life partner. Life can offer many hooks, as well as ups and downs; most of us have experienced this and learned from it. Sometimes life can offer a punch and another time we dance forward with ease. As long as you can appreciate yourself and make sure that you take care of yourself, you're helping yourself in the best way possible. You are worthy of love and that means you are also worthy of love towards yourself. Embracing and landing in who you are creates excellent conditions for many different parts of your life, including finding your Spirit Mate. When you then find each other you can, if necessary, continue the process together that you have already started. Something else that can help you on your way, and in your development, is to spend time with people who make you feel good. Relationships that are genuine and based on respect and trust, help to increase your well-being. That in itself can help you with your patience and perhaps ease your longing to find your Spirit Mate. Give yourself time and be confident that your Spirit Mate is out there.

***

We would like to give thanks for letting us share a little bit of our journey and we hope it will inspire and encourage you. For us life is really something exciting and magnificent. We value each other and we are enormously thankful that we get to share life together. There is a wealth in being Spirit Mates and we wish the same wealth for you.

With warmth, Susanne and Antti

The purpose of spirit duality

When the Spirit Mates couple begins to fulfill their common dharma, it's very important that they only merge their energies to a certain level as they otherwise will end up being one common energy with one and the same energy expression. This means that a fusion at a higher spiritual level has already started, which should not take place until the next life or later.

The purpose of spirit duality is actually not to connect with each other on a physical level, because you are already connected in spirit, most likely without knowing what the other part of your own energy looks like in the physical world. Instead, spirit duality is all about recognizing yourself and your fundamental energy constellation in another person, aka your Spirit Mate, so you can unite your energy pools and both of you can become much stronger on a personal level with the purpose of fulfilling your common dharma in this life.

So first you must recognize yourself and realize your spiritual potential, which is usually the most difficult part of finding your Spirit Mate. Then it becomes much easier for you to recognize the other half of your own energy in another person, so you can soon meet and connect with your Spirit Mate in the physical world, thereby creating a bigger "you" that consists of two bodies and one and the same spiritual intention.

To give you an overall understanding of what happens when Spirit Mates melt together in spirit to be able to raise their common energy to the next level as one big energy pool, we have added a few bullet points below that are borrowed from Anni's book "Golden Age, Golden Earth":

- Every Spirit Mates relationship is always a piece of a Spirit Mates relationship on a higher spiritual level. Once it becomes possible for people here on Earth to live with much greater consciousness than now, those who are Spirit Mates today will be merged into one joint consciousness that will then reside in a single human body. This usually takes place when one Spirit Mate dies.

- The energy of the two Spirit Mates, which will be merged into one greater consciousness in one body, will then join together with another fused Spirit Mates energy in another body, which consists of two other Spirit Mates energies that have also merged into one common Spirit Mates energy.

- All humans consist of two Spirit Mates energies which, at an earlier stage in their consciousness development and in a previous life, were split into two human bodies. So it is perfectly correct to say that you can never separate the energy of Spirit Mates, because they are destined to merge into one and the same body at a later stage in the spiritual evolution of Planet Earth.

So close and yet so far away
from each other

You and your Spirit Mate may have lived in the same neighborhood your whole life without having seen each other. The reason is that on soul level most people are not at all attracted to their own type of energy in other people. Instead, they are attracted to energy that they don't have so they can develop on a personal or consciousness level.

You can actually have been so close to each other on a physical level that you may even have had the same friends for many years, and still you have been so far away from each other on a spiritual level without knowing it.

The good part is that when you have finally recognized and succeeded in understanding the essence of your own energy at spirit level, it will not be difficult for you to spot out the qualities and skills in your Spirit Mate that will complement your personal qualities and skills. Then your Spirit Mate will most likely be just around the corner ready to meet you, because you are ready to meet him/her.

Your aura changes
when meeting your Spirit Mate

When you meet for the first time, your energies start to melt together and expand into a larger joint energy pool. It happens all by itself because both of you have a very deep and profound need to get to know each other again after being separated for so long on both the physical and the spiritual level. When this Spirit Mates Integration Process takes place, it's usually only one of you who can do things externally at a time, simply because your energies are merged into one and cannot be split again at this point in time.

When one of you needs to be extra visible in the outside world, the other partner usually has to be very introvert and silent deep inside themselves to create an overall balance in your relationship. He/she may even fall asleep everytime the most outgoing partner leaves home. Otherwise, it is not possible for any of you to go out with full joint power in the outside world. This is how things usually are when you are in the middle of your mutual integration process during the first part of your relationship, and that will be the case until the day when your respective energies have been fully merged and are in total balance.

When your respective energies have been fully merged into each other, the shape of your common big round aura will start to change into something amazing – the shape of a heart.

When your united auras have changed into the shape of a heart on a spiritual level, the two half pieces of the heart (your respective auras) will start to send out a continuous invisible energy signal to the surroundings that you have both found your Spirit Mate, and soon after your respective auras will start to separate from each other. The separation process is very important, so neither of you will have the possibility of walking around with a double-size aura while your love partner only has access to a lesser degree of your common energy pool and capacity.

It is not fair to any of you to have to hand over all your personal energy to your love partner, so they can better succeed, while you are being very low on energy yourself. However, it is actually possible to make such an agreement for one day or more where one of you will have full access to your common energy capacity. But please note that there is always an expensive price to pay for such an arrangement, because then you will have to exchange and balance your respective energies again. You won't be starting from scratch, but know that it will take quite some time for each of you and for you as a love couple to get back into balance.

The purpose of having an aura that is shaped like a half heart is, like already mentioned, to send out an invisible energy signal to your surroundings that you have found your other half, your Spirit Mate. In that way you will be separated from each other on a personal energetic level while at the same time being united on a physical and spiritual level, because after you have united your energies and split them up again, you have become identical in many ways and will therefore never be able to separate your energies again.

When a Spirit Mates couple has finally merged their energies and afterwards been individualized on a personal level, the whole Spirit Mates Integration Process, which can take years, is finished. It means that the Spirit Mates love couple now has a much larger power jointly and individually and a deeper insight into many more things than before they met, since they have both expanded their spiritual consciousness and their personal power to a level where they can now start to execute their common dharma in real life.

Later on, when the couple's bigger dharma is on its way, individual dharmas can also show up. Actually, you can have many different types of dharma and life purposes that you are supposed to fulfill during your whole lifetime.

Now it's time for you to go and find your common dharma, and we recommend that you follow the guidelines in the previous chapter *Your common life task.*

You may wonder where the heart symbol that is used everywhere on Planet Earth to illustrate love comes from, as it doesn't look like the heart that is found in the physical bodies of humans and animals, and the explanation has to be found in spirit.

In spirit, the shape of the heart represents two individualized expressions of one and the same love energy. The heart represents a totally united and balanced energy with two different minds, brains and faces that look and search for answers in different directions. Furthermore, the love couple has a mutual platform and grounding that represents their identical values in life, which is exactly what spirit duality is all about.

The Spirit Mates Integration Process is not for little boys or girls. It is a very thorough and life changing process that can be compared to when parents give birth to a newborn child in the physical world, and then multiply it by 100 or 1,000 depending on how far each of you have come in your personal development and how balanced you are. So welcome to the true world of spirit duality where the final result will forever exceed your biggest and wildest dreams ♡

Anni and Carsten

Our Love Story

The setup of our love story is very different from the 10 other love stories in this book, because we wrote our first book about Spirit Mates already back in 2003, and because we have had so many confirmations that we are meant to be together, and that sharing information about Spirit Mates is an important part of our common dharma.

Therefore, we have decided to only share essential and important experiences and details from our own relationship that will hopefully add extra value to you, and help you to understand and see an even bigger energy picture behind the concept of Spirit Mates.

For that reason, our love story may not sound as emotional and filled with love as the other love stories in this book, but don't be fooled. We have loved each other deeply from the very first day, and we still love each other more than you can imagine.

When we met, Carsten couldn't stop looking into Anni's eyes all the time. She matched exactly the picture he had deep inside, and Anni made him feel whole, so for the first time in his life, he felt unconditionally loved.

Anni loved Carsten unconditionally and still does, and she even loved him more than she loved herself, so she had several things to learn about not giving all her energy to others and helping the world without asking for anything in return. However, sharing her energy with Carsten was a pleasure and did not cause any problems at all, because he protected her in all possible ways. He was her life foundation and made so many things possible for her that she never thought would happen in her life.

For many years we were close to each other, but we couldn't see each other.

- We lived within 5 kilometers (about 3 miles) from each other and we both moved to the same area at the age of 10.

- We both sensed things about each other, but we were not able to be more specific.

- We often went to the same small mountain which was located right between our respective homes. Anni went there when she walked the family's dog, and Carsten went there to exercise.

- At the age of 12, Anni was very attracted to a boy called Carsten living close to where Carsten lived, but there was nothing more to it. It was just a sort of hint.

- We went to the same high school at the same time, but we never saw each other even though our classrooms were next to each other.

- We both met each of our love partners at a young age and where our respective love relationships lasted about six years, and we felt good where we were. There were actually many physical similarities between our respective love partners at that time and our Spirit Mate.

- We knew several of the same people, but we never met, or at least we don't remember that we have ever met. If one of us went to a party, the other part wouldn't join a party at the same place until the next time.

- So even though we were close physically, the timing and the energy were not right and ready yet. **We both needed much more life experience** before we could finally meet in the distant future and benefit from our relationship.

When we finally met at the age of 40, everything went fast.

- Our Spirit Mates Integration Process started at full speed and we got married after 9 months while also dealing with Carsten's divorce, and taking care of our four children in total (we each had two children from our respective previous relationships) and who lived in different places. On top of that Carsten had a demanding job, and we both felt that we had met 14 years later than originally "planned," so everything had to go very fast.

- We created a joint company.

- We bought a big family/business house.

- Our energies melted together and expanded into a larger joint energy pool.

- Only one of us could do things externally at a time during the Spirit Mates Integration Proccess.

- Our energies needed to get to know each other again after being apart for so long.

- Our auras were separated and united at the same time.

- Finally, the Spirit Mates Integration Process was finished, and our common dharma could begin.

Our Dharma:

- It turned out that we had so many different, comprehensive and widespread life tasks that we are supposed to act out in this life – which has been quite overwhelming for us – so we have had to be very productive and also prioritize a lot.

- For every day new and big opportunities showed up and we couldn't sit in a restaurant like most other love couples and enjoy a romantic dinner. As soon as we relaxed in each other's company, we had to write down the many ideas that came up, on all available napkins on the table.

- Carsten made a system on how to read people's energies in their faces and bodies based on Anni's clairvoyant skills, which became a part of our four element profile™ concept, that you can read about on the website: **www.fourelementprofile.com**

- It feels very natural for us to work and be creative together and we have worked together since shortly after we met each other. At that time Anni had written eight books and had started her own publishing company while at the same time she received clients for clairvoyant consultations. She lived a somewhat spiritual life and every time she earned money, she invested it in the next book project, and she didn't have any big goals in life. All she knew was that she didn't fit into the financial world where she had worked for 12.5 years back in time and it almost sucked the life out of her, because it was too structured in many ways.

- When she had given birth to her son in 1993, she quit her job and started working as an astrologer and healer, and later on as a spiritual author and clairvoyant advisor.

- Carsten, on the contrary, had a splendid business career on the fast track with IBM, Gartner and Cap Gemini, and suddenly he left it all to create a "spiritual business" together with his new wife, Anni. Everybody who knew him was totally shocked and thought he was crazy. Anni, who at that time was very sensitive to negative energies, felt everything deep inside of her body and got seriously ill.

- Later on when Carsten was occasionally focusing on "pure business" for several months or longer, working on turnarounds as well as coaching leaders in various roles, we had no resistance from the surrounding world. But as soon as it looked like he "only" supported Anni's work in the spiritual field, which is also a part of his business field, lots of resistance came up from people who are not very spiritual. Resistance also came from business partners who wanted to get access to his very powerful energy and earn extra money without taking human values so much into consideration, which is very far from our personal life values.

- It was actually very late in our Spirit Mates Integration Process that we had to fight extra hard to support and protect each other's energies in all kinds of situations and ways, which led us to write a series of Energy Self-Defense guides for Women, Men, and Love Couples etc. We had so many bad experiences within a very short period of time that it couldn't be a coincidence, and that ended up opening the door for us to release yet another common project, the Energy Self-Defense concept, which you can read about at **www.energyselfdefense.com**.

- Deep in our hearts, we knew the essence and importance of why all people should take extra good care of their own energy in daily life, and that the Energy Self-Defense concept was actually a part of our dharma as well as writing this book about Spirit Mates. As soon as we realized our important role in spreading information about these two very interesting energy universes, most of the resistance we had experienced disappeared right away.

Thank you for reading!

We really hope that you have enjoyed reading our book. *Spirit Mates* is a unique, fantastic, amazing and wonderful topic that we really want to share with the world, because everyone deserves to find their Spirit Mate and feel how it is to be united with their other half. We are sharing this knowledge through books, online courses, webinars and lectures.

Living and working together with your Spirit Mate can only lead to something bigger and better in your life, and right now we ourselves are standing in the middle of this amazing adventure.

Please send kind thoughts to all the wonderful people who shared their love stories in our book whether they are still in a physical body or in spirit. They invited you into their lives and relationships, and they shared very personal information with you that they might never have shared with anyone, if we had not asked them to.

With love and appreciation ♡

Anni & Carsten Sennov

The Authors

Anni Sennov

Anni Sennov is a clairvoyant advisor, international lecturer and the author of more than 30 books about spiritual energy, consciousness, and self-development, as well as New Time children and relationships. Several of her books have been translated into a number of languages.

Anni Sennov is the founder of AuraTransformation™, a powerful method for expanding your consciousness. She is also founder of the Aura Mediator Courses™, which take place in many countries around the world.

With her husband, Carsten Sennov, Anni is the owner of the publishing company Good Adventures Publishing, and co-owner of the management consulting and coaching company SennovPartners, where she is a consultant in the fields of personal development, energy and consciousness.

Anni and Carsten Sennov jointly created the personality type indicator four element profile™, which consists of four main energies corresponding to the four elements of Fire, Water, Earth and Air, which everyone has in different combinations and strengths. Multiple courses are offered on how to integrate, understand, read and improve communication based upon people's individual element combinations. Courses are offered to both individuals as well as businesses.

Furthermore, Anni and Carsten Sennov have developed the Energy Self-Defense concept that consists of 10+ books and online courses teaching people how to avoid losing personal energy and maintain a life in balance by using powerful mental and spiritual tools on a daily basis.

Anni Sennov was born in Denmark in 1962 and she originally began her career in the financial world. Since 1993 she has had her own practice of personal counseling. Her great strength is her ability to clairvoyantly perceive multiple relevant situations and circumstances in her clients' personality and consciousness.

Anni Sennov's work and books are mentioned in numerous magazines, newspapers, and on radio and television in many countries.

You can follow Anni Sennov on YouTube, Goodreads, LinkedIn, Google+, Twitter, Instagram and Facebook, where she has an Author Profile:

www.facebook.com/annisennov.authorprofile/

Subscribe to her English newsletter, follow her on her Golden Blog, and see her travel schedule and event calendar at **www.annisennov.com**.

Carsten Sennov

Carsten Sennov is the managing partner of SennovPartners where he works as a consultant and advisor for business leaders and their teams.

Responsible for SennovPartners' franchise-based spiritual training businesses, he oversees the continued international expansion which today covers many countries in Europe, the USA, and Japan.

As CEO and co-owner of Good Adventures Publishing, he is responsible for publishing and selling the company's books worldwide.

Carsten is married to Anni Sennov and has co-authored 10+ of the 30+ books she has written on spirituality and personal development.

He is the main author of "Be a Conscious Leader in Your Own Life," which includes a description of the four element profile™ personality type indicator, which the couple has jointly developed.

In 2018 and 2019 Carsten Sennov worked on a major transformation as Director of Operations & Execution for Bisnode International Region, turning 15 countries into one Region.

In April 2017, the couple launched the Energy Self-Defense concept and the first three books at a major event in New York, having one-on-one dialogues with 50 American journalists.

In 2012-13, Carsten was the EMEA (Europe, the Middle East and Africa) contact person for Essess Inc. – an MIT (Massachusetts Institute of Technology) spin-out in Cleantech.

In 2011 the couple started the course company four element profile™, where Carsten is the managing partner. Courses are offered in collaboration with trained associated partners in the Nordic countries and in the USA. Courses are also available online.

Most of 2010 Carsten Sennov worked on a major turnaround for the Danish division of a world leading credit management services company.

Most of 2008 he worked for Vaekstfonden, the Danish State investment fund, with an incubation project within the Cleantech area.

In 2006 he worked on a major improvement program for a large Telecom provider.

In most of 2004 he worked on a major consulting assignment, improving a corporation in the Service Industry.

Carsten Sennov was Deputy CEO at Capgemini Denmark, where he was employed from 1999 to 2003. Here he was also directly responsible for Capgemini's largest division – the Technology Services division – as well as Deputy CEO for this division in the Nordic region.

During the period 1991-1998 he worked for Gartner; the last four years being based in Sydney, Australia, where he was Operations Director at Gartner Measurement Asia Pacific.

He has also worked in product and sales roles for Gartner and IBM.

Carsten Sennov has been a sportsman at an elite level and has traveled extensively. His exploits included sailing across the Atlantic Ocean in a riverboat and later on, traveling six months in the Australian Outback. He has worked very extensively in personal development.

Follow Carsten and read testimonials etc. on his LinkedIn profile:
www.linkedin.com/in/carstensennov

Visit our websites:

www.annisennov.com

www.carstensennov.com

www.sennovpartners.com

www.energyselfdefense.com

www.fourelementprofile.com

www.good-adventures.com

www.sennovpartnersacademy.com

Follow our Spirit Mates groups and profiles on social media:

Facebook: www.facebook.com/groups/spiritmates/

Instagram: www.instagram.com/spiritmates/

Anni & Carsten Sennov's Authorship

Books in English written by Anni Sennov

- Golden Age, Golden Earth
- Balance on All Levels with the Crystal and Indigo Energies
- The Crystal Human and the Crystallization Process Part I
- The Crystal Human and the Crystallization Process Part II
- Karma-free in the New Time
- Crystal Children, Indigo Children and Adults of the Future
- Love, Sex and Attraction – A Short Guide to a Successful Relationship

Books in English written by Anni & Carsten Sennov

- SPIRIT MATES – How to Find Your Soul Mate Version 2.0
  Your Ultimate Love Partner
- Spirit Mates – The New Time Relationship
- Energy Self-Defense for Women
- Energy Self-Defense for Men
- Energy Self-Defense for Young Adults
- Energy Self-Defense for Love Couples
- Energy Self-Defense for Sick People and Their Relatives
- Get Your Power Back Now!
- The Little Energy Guide 1

Buy their books here:

Amazon, Barnes & Noble and other online bookstores

Titles in all languages, and titles for books that are currently out-of-stock can be found here:

www.annisennov.com/profile/anni-sennovs-authorship/

For more information visit www.annisennov.com